Famous Biographies for Young People

FAMOUS NEGRO
ENTERTAINERS
of Stage, Screen, and TV

OTHER BOOKS BY CHARLEMAE ROLLINS

Christmas Gif'
They Showed the Way
Famous American Negro Poets

FAMOUS NEGRO ENTERTAINERS
of Stage, Screen, and TV

by Charlemae Rollins

ILLUSTRATED

Dodd, Mead & Company · New York

This book is affectionately dedicated
to my mother,
Mrs. Birdie Tucker Hill, aged 95,
who listens with pride and enjoyment to
all the young Negro entertainers

ACKNOWLEDGMENTS

GRATEFUL ACKNOWLEDGMENT is made to the following friends for editorial assistance and help in research:

Margaret Taylor Burroughs of The Negro History Museum, for use of the following photographs: Nat "King" Cole, Sammy Davis, Jr., Eartha Kitt, and Sidney Poitier, and for checking the historical material.

Margaret Thomsen Raymond, author of teen-age novels for girls, for editorial help.

To the following librarians in Chicago for providing reference help and biographical data: Mrs. Ellyn Askins Hill, Librarian, Hiram Kelly Branch, Chicago; Miss Marie C. Will, Supervisor, Work with Children, Central Library of Chicago; Miss Irene A. Watkins, Assistant Librarian, George C. Hall Library; Mrs. Dorothy C. Evans, Children's Librarian, Hall Branch Library.

And to Mrs. Josephine Glover Sanders, who patiently checked and rechecked the manuscript and typed all the many versions of it.

And to my husband, Joseph, who patiently gave his time for all the details I needed for this work.

Charlemae Rollins

CONTENTS

PHOTOGRAPHIC SUPPLEMENT

MARIAN ANDERSON

IRA ALDRIDGE

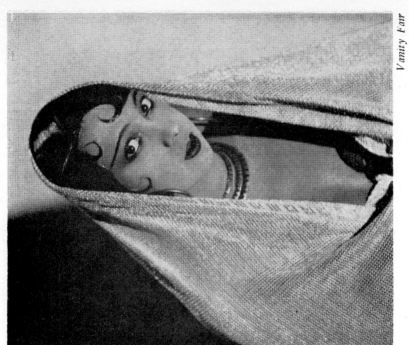

JOSEPHINE BAKER

LOUIS "SATCHMO" ARMSTRONG

NAT "KING" COLE

New York Times

HARRY BELAFONTE

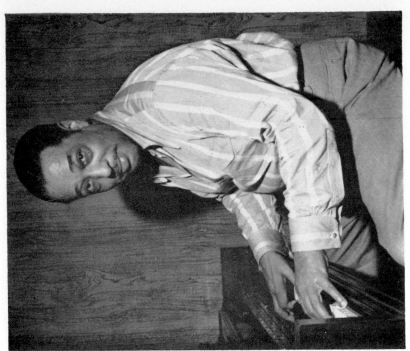

"Duke" Ellington

Sammy Davis, Jr.

EARTHA KITT

LENA HORNE

LEONTYNE PRICE

SIDNEY POITIER

Paramount Productions, Inc.

BILL "BOJANGLES" ROBINSON

PAUL ROBESON

"Bert" Williams

"Fats" Waller

INTRODUCTION

Long before their appearance on the stage, Negroes were amusing spectators with their own songs and dances on the plantation. They were also using their musical talents in their fight for freedom. The cruel overseers often forced the workers to sing as they toiled. He ordered them to "make a noise there!" and "bear a hand."

Frederick Douglass, eminent Negro writer and abolitionist, writes in his *Autobiography:* "Slaves were expected to sing as well as work. There was generally more or less singing among teamsters at all times. It was a means of telling the overseer in the distance where they were and what they were about. While on the way they would make the grand old woods for miles around reverberate with their wild and plaintive notes. They were indeed both merry and sad. Child as I was, these wild songs greatly depressed my spirits."

Harriet Tubman, the famous slave woman who helped to liberate more than two hundred slaves by stealing them from their plantations by night and guiding them North to freedom, with the help of the white and Negro abolitionists, tells in her autobiography that she gave the signals to the slaves by singing such songs as "Steal Away to Jesus," as she moved quietly from cabin to cabin in the dead of night. This was her way of notifying those who were to accompany her on the trips. Later they celebrated by singing "Free at Last, Free at Last! Thank God Almighty I'm Free at Last!" These songs are now among the great spirituals of the world.

The plantation songs were used interchangeably for church as "Revival shouts," for burial songs, for hymns of praise and consolation, as well as for signals in the Underground Railroad era. These hymns and sorrow songs were later made famous by the Fisk University Jubilee Singers.

This group of eleven students, six young women and five young men, along with a teacher, began making tours on October 6, 1871, under the direction of George L. White. On November 15, they sang at Oberlin before the National Council of Congregational Churches, and were advised to "push on to the East." They toured the New England cities with little money and much faith, singing their spirituals and slave songs. After many months of hardships, they embarked for England. There they were received everywhere with great favor; and sang their slave songs before the Queen as well as other notables. Within three years, this troupe returned to the United States, bringing with them a fund of over one hundred thousand dollars, which built the fine Memorial Hall at Fisk University.

Some of the most successful of the early singers were women. One of the first was Elizabeth Taylor Greenfield, commonly known as The Black Swan because of her dark beauty and graceful demeanor. She was born in Natchez, Mississippi, in 1809, brought to Philadelphia when she was only one year old, and reared by a Quaker lady, Mrs. Greenfield, whose religious beliefs found music and singing "sinful." One day, after she had heard that Elizabeth was being taught to sing by some of the young white people, Mrs. Greenfield asked, "Elizabeth, is it true that thee is learning music and can play the guitar?" When Elizabeth admitted that this was indeed true, she said, "Go get the guitar and let me hear thee sing." Elizabeth brought her guitar and sang for her benefactor, who afterward smiled and said, "Elizabeth, whatever thee wants thee shall have."

Elizabeth was allowed to continue her musical studies and later gave concerts in many of the large churches. In 1844, following Mrs. Greenfield's death, Elizabeth went to Buffalo, New York, to continue her musical education. In October, 1851, she sang before the Buffalo Musical Association and was received with great enthusiasm, her voice being compared to that of Jenny Lind, then known as the "Swedish Nightingale." She was invited to sing in New York, Boston, and other cities in the East.

Elizabeth later went abroad armed with letters from enthusiastic friends in America. She arrived in London on April 16, 1853, where she met Harriet Beecher Stowe, author of *Uncle Tom's Cabin*, who was visiting abroad at the time. Mrs. Stowe introduced her to many music lovers there, among them Sir George Smart, organist of the Chapel Royal. He invited Miss Greenfield to sing for his friends, and this led to an invitation to give a command performance for Her Majesty Queen Victoria at Buckingham Palace on May 10, 1864. She returned to America in July, 1864, and opened a studio to help struggling young Negroes achieve success in music. She died in April, 1876.

Sisseretta Jones, whose maiden name was Matilda S. Joyner, popularly known as Black Patti, was born in 1863 in Portsmouth, Virginia. When she was quite young, her parents moved to Providence, Rhode Island. There, at the age of fifteen, she began her piano lessons. As she was a bright pupil, her teacher encouraged her to take lessons in voice, and when she was eighteen years old, she enrolled at the New England Conservatory of Music in Boston. She advanced so rapidly that she was asked to sing at a benefit concert for the aid of the Parnell Defense Fund where the audience numbered more than five thousand. This was such a success she decided on a career as a professional singer.

Black Patti first went to the West Indies, where she was enormously well liked. She was showered with lavish gifts of jewels—pearls, rubies, and diamonds. The President of the Republic made a presentation to her of a purse of five hundred dollars in gold. Upon her return she toured all the large cities of the United States and sang at Madison Square Garden in April, 1892, as the principal soloist.

President Harrison invited her to sing at a reception at the White House in September of the same year. She sang arias, ballads, both comic and sentimental, songs which told of the sorrows of her people as well as the songs of joy. She organized a singing group known as "Black Patti's Troubadours" which toured the United States for nineteen years, singing operatic airs and musical comedy songs. In her years of retirement in Providence, Rhode Island, she lived quietly, devoted to her church work and other good causes. She died in 1933.

Men also made their presence felt in the field of entertainment. One of the most significant of his day was Thomas Green Bethune, known as "Blind Tom," who was a slave child born blind on May 25, 1849. He was one of the earliest Negro entertainers to gain international fame. He was said to have one of the most unusual gifts known to music—the gift of "absolute pitch," together with an unerring ear and a most astonishing memory.

Blind Tom heard a piano played for the first time when he was about four years of age and he immediately fell in love with this instrument. He felt it, touched it all over, and then sat down and began playing it. Later he could accurately play the entire selection of any music he had just heard. He played the most difficult passages from Beethoven, Chopin, Mendelssohn, Donizetti, and others, after hearing them only one time. His power of retention and reproduction of sounds was phenomenal. He was ranked among the unique prodigies known to musical history, and performed in the music halls of London, Paris, Edinburgh, and many other European cities.

Blind Tom, at the height of his career, offered a list of eighty-two numbers from which to select a program. To this he invited anyone to perform any selection of music, the more difficult the piece, the more acceptable to Tom; he would immediately sit down at the piano and produce the whole of what he had just heard!

All who heard him were astonished at his performances. He traveled extensively in Europe as well as the United States, and had a repertoire of seven thousand pieces which he had learned from having heard them played to him. All these he remembered and played with precision and accuracy again and again. He died in 1908.

The Negro as a factor in American entertainment stems from the plantation singer, dancer, and jester who performed for their masters, at the same time deriving pleasure for themselves from their art. They have a physical beauty of movement, natural distinction, and grace. Musically they have rhythm, real resonance, excellent pitch, superb enunciation, and never look bored or out of place on the stage.

Negroes have become a composite character in American life. They have taken and have given culturally. Their musical preferences and sense of rhythm have been the result of environmental conditioning, and their ideals, feelings, and values are products of the American culture modified by a transmission of it through themselves. The American Negro has given great joy to the field of light entertainment and has added much understanding to the areas of serious make-believe as well.

IRA ALDRIDGE

Actor

[1807–1867]

IRA ALDRIDGE, America's first great Negro actor, was born in New York City in 1807. His father, a Senegal chieftain, had been brought by missionaries to the United States, where he later became a Presbyterian minister.

Ira attended the African Free School established in New York for free Negroes long before there was any such institution for white children. In his early years Ira developed a fascination for the theatre. He did bit parts in productions of the African Theatre on Grove Street in New York. Later he held a night job at the Chatham Theatre, where he could listen to the actors backstage and take part in amateur theatricals.

After finishing his preliminary education, Aldridge attended Schenectady College for a short time until his father decided to send the teen-aged boy to the University of Glasgow, Scotland, where a number of the antislavery leaders had studied. He wanted his son to study medicine.

Although Ira made records for scholarship, winning prizes and a medal for Latin composition, he could not get the theatre out of his system. After a year and a half in Scotland, he went to London and plunged wholeheartedly into a theatrical career. Through dogged perseverance, he was allowed to play Othello in an East End theatre, where his performance was so fine that he was well launched on his way.

Londoners were fascinated by this handsome, black young man with the powerful, thrilling voice, whose repertoire ranged from penny thrillers to Shakespeare with equal gusto. After touring England from one end to the other, Aldridge finally won the plaudits of the discriminating critics of London's West End theatres. Soon thereafter, he went to Dublin, Ireland, where he opened in *Othello* and quickly became a sensation. Here he was seen by the great English actor, Edmund Kean, who paid him the ultimate compliment of asking Aldridge to play his "Iago." Their production opened in London at Covent Garden in 1833 and is reported to have been one of the greatest presentations ever. They played together in England and on the continent for many years and developed an artistic and personal friendship of warmth and intimacy.

For twenty years Aldridge was an established figure in the English theatre. His repertoire included the great classics of England such as Hamlet, Lear, Macbeth, as well as plays which contained more traditional roles for colored actors. As an American and as a Negro, Aldridge showed the classic-conscious, Shakespeare-proud English how great emotions could be projected simply and with profound feeling. In 1825, he traveled abroad, where he was accepted with triumphant acclaim. Here, he was embraced by the great men of Europe, honored by the Kings of Sweden, Prussia, and Austria. He was decorated by the city of Berlin, and Berne, Switzerland, presented him with the Maltese Cross, the medal of merit. The actor was also elected to a variety of learned societies.

Ira had once and for all established the fact that if a white man could play Negro parts, a Negro could, with even greater effectiveness, broaden his scope and include any part which suited his talent. He went to Russia and was such a success that the French actor Gatier, traveling there at the same time, said, "Aldridge is the lion of all St. Petersburg." While there, the students took the horses from his carriage and drew him to his hotel. The intelligentsia of the city struggled to "kiss his noble black hand."

Aldridge loved Russia and referred to it as his second home. He returned there five times within the next ten years. He and the famous Ukrainian poet-artist, Chevshenko, became great friends, and this artist painted the actor's portrait in 1858.

In 1865, Ira made his last London appearance in *Othello*, with Mrs. Kendall playing his "Desdemona." He numbered among his admirers and intimate friends: Alexandre Dumas, author of *The Three Musketeers;* the Count and Countess Tolstoy, who wrote about him with great warmth and admiration; Jenny Lind, known as the Swedish Nightingale, and Hans Christian Andersen, who was inspired to write his only successful play, *The Mulatto*, after having seen Aldridge perform on the stage.

Ira's successes include, not only *Othello*, which he played in London and on his tour of the Continent in Germany, Austria, Sweden, and Russia, but also the role of Christophe, the liberator of Haiti, in *The Death of Christophe*.

When the Civil War had ended and slavery was destroyed in the United States, Aldridge was approaching sixty years of age. He talked with friends and his manager about returning to the land of his birth, and plans were set under way. Meanwhile, the actor returned to the Continent for another tour of Russia, but he was not destined to reach his second home. In Lodz, Poland, where he was an honored citizen, he was taken ill and died on August 7, 1867. A civic funeral was arranged and many great men of Europe were among his mourners. Ira Aldridge was laid to rest in Lodz, Poland. A seat in the Shakespeare Memorial Theatre at Stratford-on-Avon was dedicated to his memory with a bronze plate inscribed with his name.

MARIAN ANDERSON

Contralto

[1908–   ]

W HEN MARIAN ANDERSON made her first "public" appearance singing at a church building fund affair at the age of
eight years, handbills were passed out with the inscription
"COME AND HEAR THE BABY CONTRALTO." She had been sent
to the store by her mother to buy bread and became so excited when she saw the handbill bearing her name, she bought
potatoes instead. This was the first step on the road to fame
which lay ahead for the famous singer.

Marian, the oldest of three daughters, was born on Webster
Street in South Philadelphia, Pennsylvania, on February 27,
1908. Her father, John Anderson, was employed by day at
the Reading Terminal Market in the refrigerator room, and
often did odd jobs selling coal and ice. Her mother, Annie,
had been a schoolteacher in Virginia, but gave up her career
soon after her marriage.

Marian recalls that her childhood was a very happy one.
She and her sisters had toys, mostly dolls, and played the
games common to all children. She enjoyed running errands
for her mother and grandmother. Her parents were very
religious, and her father took pride in his work as a Special

Officer in the Union Baptist Church. He often took Marian with him to church on Sunday mornings before her little sisters, Ethel and Alyce, were old enough to go, and by the time she was six years old, her father enrolled Marian in the junior choir of the church.

Marian looked forward to the choir each Sunday. She loved to sing and learned the verses of many of the hymns by heart. She made the acquaintance of the other boys and girls in the choir, and became good friends with one little girl, Viola Johnson, who later sang a duet with her for the Sunday school. The song was so well received and the director of the choir was so pleased with the sweet voices of Marian and Viola that he asked them to sing it for the Sunday morning worship service.

When Marian was still a small child, her father had an accident where he worked. Something fell and struck his head, making him quite ill for some time. The doctors said he had a tumor on the brain, and he never recovered from the accident. Shortly after Christmas in 1918, Mr. Anderson died. Marian's mother had to move out of the house in which they were living to the home of Mr. Anderson's mother and sister. Marian continued singing in the choir, but she missed her father very much.

By the time she was fourteen, Marian was singing in both the senior and junior choirs, and was often given solo parts in the anthems. The members of the Union Baptist Church began to take an interest in Marian's voice, as they felt that it was quite unusual. They decided to raise money for her to take singing lessons, and gave a number of concerts for this purpose. The money that was raised was put into a trust fund called "Marian Anderson's Future," because her first teacher refused to take any pay for her lessons.

Marian attended William Penn High School after she was graduated from grammar school. There she took a commercial course with the hope of getting a job as a typist when she finished high school. But she still studied music and sang whenever the opportunity presented itself, taking part in the school chorus and singing occasional solos. At one of the school assemblies where Marian had a solo part when visitors were present, they were so impressed with her voice that she was asked to come into the principal's office to speak with them. Marian said, "I have forgotten the principal's name, but I remember the name of the stranger in the office, Dr. Rohrer, who asked the principal why I was taking shorthand and typing when I should have a college preparatory course and do as much as possible in music."

She was transferred to South Philadelphia High School, where a more extensive music program was offered. The principal there, Dr. Lucy Wilson, took a special interest in Marian and often arranged programs so that she could be heard. While in her second year of high school, a distinguished Negro actor, John Thomas Butler, heard Marian and sent her to a voice teacher, Mary S. Patterson. This teacher also refused to take any pay for her singing lessons, so the trust fund was saved for more advanced training when she became older.

When she was fifteen years old Marian sang a group of songs alone at the School Convention in Harrisburg, and many people in the State of Pennsylvania heard her unusual voice. After her graduation from high school, the Philadelphia Choral Society, a Negro group, sponsored her further study with a famous contralto singer and teacher, Agnes

Reifsnyder. In 1925, when Marian was seventeen years old, her high school principal, Dr. Lucy Wilson, helped her to meet Giuseppe Boghetti, another renowned teacher, who, after hearing her sing, entered Marian's name in a New York Philharmonic competition along with three hundred other young singers.

She won first place in the contest and was presented at the Lewisohn Stadium in New York, accompanied by the New York Philharmonic Orchestra. This was a great triumph for the poor Negro girl from Philadelphia! It gave her wide publicity, but she was not able to make much money. The people who heard her often said, "A wonderful voice; it's just too bad she's a Negro." Marian gave many concerts, most of them in Negro churches and colleges in the South.

Each year the Union Baptist Church in Philadelphia gave a gala concert featuring a celebrated artist. When Marian returned from her concerts, she was asked to take part in the grand affair. She learned that the famous Negro tenor, Roland Hayes, was to be the featured artist and she was thrilled. Roland Hayes listened attentively when Marian sang and was impressed with her voice. Marian sat entranced while Mr. Hayes performed. When the program was over, Roland Hayes asked to speak with her family about her voice and special training for her. He talked with her mother and grandmother, suggesting that Marian be sent to a boarding school to study music. Her grandmother firmly refused to allow Marian to leave the family circle in order to study. Marian was quite heartbroken for a while, because Roland Hayes was her idol, and to think that he had taken an interest in her! She later said, "In all those schoolgirl years, one experience stands out in my memory—the gala concert when I appeared on the same platform with Roland Hayes."

Even with a voice that Arturo Toscanini said "comes once in a century," Miss Anderson found it difficult to obtain singing engagements in the United States. In 1930, she received a Rosenwald Fellowship and went to England and the continent of Europe for further study and to perfect her pronunciation of Italian, French, and German.

While there, Marian made her debut in Berlin. A prominent Scandinavian concert manager read about the scheduled concert and sent two friends to hear the American Negro girl with a Scandinavian name. One of them was Kosti Vehanen, who became Marian Anderson's accompanist, and they traveled together for many years. He later wrote a full-length biography of Miss Anderson.

She was invited to sing in several Scandinavian countries, where the people loved her because Marian learned to sing in their own languages: Swedish, Finnish, and Norwegian. Later she sang before King Gustaf in Stockholm, King Christian in Copenhagen, and was invited to the home of the great Finnish composer, Sibelius, where she sang for him. The following year, 1931, she gave a concert in Paris which was followed by overwhelming successes all over Europe. It was in Europe that Marian Anderson was first acclaimed as "the greatest singer in the world."

Although she left the United States discouraged by the barriers of racial discrimination, after her successes abroad Marian was invited to give a large concert in Carnegie Hall in New York City. She was excited and thrilled to be returning in triumph to her homeland. Marian had made great preparations for her first concert, but just before the boat landed in New York, she slipped on the deck of the ship and broke her ankle. She refused to allow her manager to cancel the concert and asked that no one be told of the accident.

The night of the concert, Marian Anderson wore a beautiful long dress in order that the audience should not see that her foot was in a cast. She asked the stagehands to keep the curtains closed while she placed herself in the curve of the grand piano, so that part of her weight could rest on the instrument. In this way Miss Anderson sang the entire concert on one foot!

In 1936, Marian was invited to the White House to visit President and Mrs. Franklin D. Roosevelt, and on July 2, 1939, Mrs. Roosevelt presented Marian with the Spingarn Medal, which is given annually by The National Association for the Advancement of Colored People to the American Negro who has "made the highest achievement during the preceding year in any field of endeavor." In 1940 Miss Anderson won the Bok Award for her contribution to music.

On July 24, 1943, Marian Anderson was married to Orpheus H. Fischer, an architect. They bought a beautiful farm in Connecticut, where Marian finds peace and quiet after her many concerts.

When, in 1939, the Daughters of the American Revolution refused to allow Miss Anderson to give a concert in Constitution Hall, Harold Ickes, then Secretary of the Interior, and Mrs. Eleanor Roosevelt, wife of the President of the United States, arranged an open-air concert for her. And so, before 75,000 persons on Easter Sunday, on the steps of the Lincoln Memorial in Washington, D.C., Marian Anderson was given the honors she should have had long before from her fellow countrymen.

Marian Anderson appeared on the stage of the Metropolitan Opera House in 1955, the first of her race to perform there. As a result, talented persons of all races and nationalities are now welcomed there. During 1957, the State Department sent her on a good-will tour of the world so that the peoples of Japan, India, and the countries of Africa might hear and honor this wonderful and gifted American. Miss Anderson appeared before the King of Thailand, who broke precedent by rising from his throne to greet her. She was the only foreigner ever invited to speak before the Gandhi Memorial in Old Delhi.

In 1958, Marian Anderson became a United States delegate to the 13th U.N. General Assembly. With her own funds, she has established the Marian Anderson Foundation to help other talented young musicians finish their training and obtain the advantages of European and advanced studies, for which she worked so long and so hard.

During the inaugurations of President Dwight D. Eisenhower and President John F. Kennedy, Miss Anderson was given the great honor of singing "The Star-Spangled Banner". She has been awarded honorary degrees by ten colleges and universities, and has been decorated by almost as many foreign countries.

Critics have called hers "a voice of many rewarding timbres —clear and silvery in the soft upper tones, full and warm in the lower register." On Easter Sunday, 1965, at her last American concert at Carnegie Hall, Marian Anderson announced her intention to retire.

LOUIS "SATCHMO" ARMSTRONG

Trumpet Player

[1900–   ]

Louis ARMSTRONG, affectionately known as "Satchmo," was born in New Orleans, Louisiana, on July 4, 1900. His father, Willie Armstrong, was a laborer in a turpentine factory, and his mother, Mary Ann, cooked for a family in the French Quarter. Louis's sister, Beatrice, was born two years later. Since both parents worked, Louis and his little sister were cared for by their grandmother, Josephine Albert.

When Louis was five years old, his mother and father were separated, and he and Beatrice went to live with their grandmother. A few years later, his mother remarried and Louis went to live with her on Perdido Street in New Orleans. He attended the Fisk School and made friends with the children who had nicknames, such as "Sweet Child," "Little Mack," and "Big Nose." Louis's wide, grinning mouth and large lips soon won him the nickname of "Dippermouth"; later he was called "Satchelmouth," which was shortened to the well-known "Satchmo."

The neighborhood was full of music. There were many honky-tonks and music halls on the streets. Louis would stand beneath the windows of one of the cabarets for hours stomping his foot in time with the music. At the age of seven he started selling papers for a news vender. He could be heard far down the street as he stood on the corner yelling, "Paper, paper, latest paper!" He often left his post to follow bands as they paraded in the street, marching to the beat of the music.

When "Satchmo" was nine years old, he left school for a full-time job working on Konowski's coal truck, earning seventy-five cents to a dollar a day, including tips. He continued to listen to the music coming from the dance halls in the neighborhood every chance he got, and longed to play an instrument and become a musician.

The turning point in Louis's life came when he was thirteen years old. He found an old .38 caliber pistol in his mother's trunk and took it out with him. He and some friends were standing on a corner when a cat ran across the street. One of his friends yelled, "Get him, Satchmo!" Louis pulled the gun from his pocket and began shooting at the cat. Urged on by his friends, Louis began shooting up and down the street in Wild West fashion. The sheriff came and arrested him and he was sentenced to a term in the Colored Waifs' Home. Of this incident "Satchmo" says, "I do believe that my whole success goes back to that time when I was arrested as a wayward boy at the age of thirteen, because I had to quit running around and begin to learn something. Most of all, I began to learn music."

While in the Waifs' Home, Louis started playing the tambourine in the institution's band, and was later transferred to the drums, and eventually became bugler. He blew his bugle each morning to wake the other members of the Home. Before he left the Home, Louis was playing the cornet and had been made the leader of the band.

After a year and a half, Louis left the Waifs' Home and went back to his job on the coal truck. Since he was fifteen years old, he was given the job of driver, and there seemed very little chance of his ever playing a horn again. He had to be up very early and worked until late at night. He was often so tired he could not listen to the music coming from the dance halls.

One night the cornet player in Prince Harry's Cabaret failed to appear for work, and Louis Armstrong got his first chance to play in public. He was offered the job and played on a borrowed cornet. "Satchmo" was an immediate success, for he was so happy to be playing in a band again, he put his whole heart into every piece. And so Louis worked at night in the Cabaret and still kept his job on the coal truck during the day.

It was while delivering coal in the French Quarter one day that Louis met the great musician, King Oliver, who became his friend. Oliver gave him one of his old cornets and got him engagements in some of the better night clubs. Best of all, he taught Louis something of his own technique and encouraged him to spend more time playing the horn. When King Oliver left New Orleans for Chicago, he invited Louis to join him.

So, in 1922, twenty-two-year-old Louis "Satchmo" Armstrong moved from New Orleans to Chicago and became a member of the jazz band of his friend and early teacher. Oliver's "Creole Jazz Band" was one of the group that helped the spread of jazz music during the 1920's. Armstrong soon learned the so-called "Chicago style" of jazz, and before long was outstripping his teacher.

In 1924, Louis went to New York and joined the Fletcher Henderson Band, and soon became its featured soloist. Musicians and composers flocked to hear him and many tried to imitate his style, which almost from the beginning affected the whole of jazz music. But Chicago had won Louis's heart, so after two years with the Henderson Band in New York, he went back to Chicago and joined Erskine Tate's orchestra at the Vendome Theatre.

While at the Vendome, "Satchmo" organized his own band, called "Louis Armstrong's Hot Five," and began making records. By this time he had abandoned the cornet for the trumpet and his fame on this instrument was spreading. His technique was more precise than had appeared before, his musical ideas were more consistent, and his rhythm was surer. Until 1929, Louis had, in effect, been reinterpreting jazz as he found it. He now began to alter one note here, five notes there; he delayed the phrase, and made sweet music out of anything he played.

In his 1930 version of "Sweethearts on Parade" and his 1933 version of "Basin Street Blues," Armstrong clearly outlined the phrasing and rhythmic manner of modern jazz. He was also capable of pure melodic invention with little or no reference to a theme, as in "When It's Sleepy Time Down South" and "I Can't Give You Anything but Love." His singing in the "frog croaking" voice made him famous for his "scat" singing—a form of talking in a singsong.

Although Louis loved Chicago, he did not remain there for long, for his fame as a trumpeter had spread far and wide. After a number of road tours and a few months in Hollywood, he left for Europe, playing in London, Paris, and Scotland. "Satchmo" met with wild acclaim on the Continent, where his artistry and warm personality endeared him to thousands of music lovers.

In 1954, Louis toured Japan and here the "King of Jazz" received a royal welcome. He had the most thrilling experience of his life in 1956 when he visited Africa, the land of his ancestors. Thousands of Ghanians welcomed Armstrong "home," and he won their hearts with his music and superb showmanship.

"Satchmo" has put at least a thousand numbers on wax, among them some of his best-known recordings: "Shine," "Tiger Rag," "Ain't Misbehavin'," "Lazy River," and "Georgia on My Mind." He has written more than twenty tunes and is a member of the American Society of Composers, Authors, and Publishers.

Although Armstrong's peak years are full of excellent recordings, his recent "comeback" is spectacular. His banjo-and-trumpet treatment of "Hello, Dolly" became the number-one hit with teen-agers as well as adults. More than half a million copies have been sold. In addition to this, "I Still Get Jealous" and "Blueberry Hill," both Armstrong single records, are moving up fast into first place with music lovers.

In 1960, Louis "Satchmo" Armstrong was selected by the United States State Department to travel as a good-will ambassador to Europe, Russia, and Africa, where he was warmly and enthusiastically received. His powerful, driving trumpet style became known throughout the world.

Armstrong has become more and more the genial "Satchmo," the grand old man, the engaging entertainer and night club performer, the jazz trumpeter, who is successful with almost any audience.

JOSEPHINE BAKER
Dancer-Singer
[1906–   ]

THE "TOAST OF PARIS" was the name given to a young
song and dance artist who starred in the famous Folies-
Bergère. She was Josephine Baker, who was born in St. Louis,
Missouri, on June 3, 1906, the oldest child of Louis and Cary
(Smith) Baker. There were three other children in the family
—her brother Richard, and sisters Margaret and Ellie May.
Her father, Louis, was a traveling merchant who was not
with his family much, and her mother, Cary, had to help support the family by taking in laundry.

Josephine left school at the age of eight to work as a
kitchen helper, maid, and baby-sitter in private homes in
order to bring added support for her younger brother and sisters. She returned to school, however, when she was ten years
old and enjoyed the accounts of kings and queens in her history books. Her favorite childhood pastime was to mas-
querade in adult clothing and make up basement theatricals.

When she was in her early teens, Josephine went to the
local vaudeville house at least once a week in order to watch
the dancers. She practiced until she had learned most of the
steps she had seen the dancers do, and while still in elementary

39

school, began dancing part-time in a chorus line on the vaudeville stage.

At sixteen, Josephine joined a traveling troupe in Philadelphia, where she was then living with her grandmother. The troupe had many one-night engagements in small towns, and her dancing ability and personality attracted the attention of all who saw the reviews. When she left the troupe, Miss Baker went to New York, where she was given a chance as one of the dancers in the chorus of Noble Sissle's musical comedy, *Shuffle Along*, which was playing at the Music Hall. Josephine had been placed at the end of the line of dancers, and drew applause from the audience for her natural flair for improvisation and imitation.

In 1924, Sissle and Blake wrote a show called *The Chocolate Dandies*, which included an excellent chorus of dancing girls. Josephine Baker was one of the girls in the line, and she stood out because of her flashing eyes and beautiful body, which seemed to be made for dancing. She did a little trick of pushing her head forward on her neck just as some animal might have done when he scented food ahead. This fascinated the audiences, and her name began to appear more and more in print due to her naturalness and uncanny power of projecting her personality and talent.

Within a year, in October, 1925, Miss Baker was offered a major dancing part in *La Revue Negre*, an American production that opened at the Theatre des Champs Élysées in Paris, France. With this review, "le jazz hot" had invaded France for the first time and Josephine Baker became the toast of Paris.

When her manager talked her into incorporating speech and song into her performances, she came into full flower.

Her quivering, low-pitched, husky voice, accompanied by her flashing smile, added to her charm. The elaborate costumes she wore soon became her trademark. The critics were unanimous in their praise of the young entertainer who changed from a simple eccentric dancer to a complete artist who became master of all her tools. Because of her singing and dancing ability and her charming personality, Josephine Baker was starred in the famous Folies-Bergère, where her name went up on the marquee in blazing neon.

Andre Levinson, Europe's most distinguished critic of the classic dance, said of her performance, "Josephine Baker dances like a sinuous idol that enslaves and excites mankind. Thanks to her carnal magnificence, her exhibition comes close to pathos. It was she who led the spell-bound drummer and the fascinated saxophonist in the harsh rhythm of the blues. It was as though the jazz, catching on the wing the vibrations of this mad body, were interpreting word by word its fantastic monologue. The music is born from the dance, and what a dance! Certain of Miss Baker's poses had the compelling potency of the finest examples of Negro sculpture. It was no longer a grotesque dancing girl who stood before the audience, but the black Venus that haunted Baudelaire."

Miss Baker was making her third film in France when World War II broke out. She became a Red Cross volunteer and traveled wherever her services were needed: to Southwest France, Spain, Portugal; to Algiers, North Africa, and back to Marseilles, France. After the liberation of France in August, 1944, Miss Baker returned to Paris, which she had made her home, and entertained at the Theatre aux Armées. She continued to star regularly in the Folies-Bergère during the postwar years.

In 1947, Josephine married Jo Bouillon, the French orchestra leader. She made many international tours, which included visits to the United States on several occasions. In August, 1963, she came to America to participate in the Civil Rights march on Washington, and in October, 1963, she appeared in Carnegie Hall for a benefit performance for Civil Rights.

Josephine Baker has attracted much attention in recent years by her international experiment in brotherhood. She has adopted and is raising eleven orphaned children of varied racial origins at her French chateau. They are Akio (Korean); Louis (Colombian); Jarri (Finnish); Jean Claude (French); Jannot (Japanese); Moses (Israeli); Brahim (Arab); Marianne (French), the only girl; Mara (Venezuelan Indian); Cokoffi (African); and Noel (French). She and her husband adopted these children, "to prove to doubters our conviction that human beings can live together without religious or racial hatred or discrimination." Each child is privately tutored, with consideration for his or her religious and cultural background, and although they are legally adopted, Miss Baker says they are to return to their native lands when they reach the age of eighteen.

Miss Baker, still beautiful in her sixties, made a triumphant return to the American stage after an absence of twelve years. Her performance met with cheers, bravos, and several standing ovations. John S. Wilson, a reviewer for the *New York Times*, stated of her, "It was completely Miss Baker's evening. She brought the hall alive with excitement the moment she stepped upon the stage, and that excitement never diminished until she finally retired after receiving a roaring tribute of approval that brought the entire audience to its feet and led many to rush to the footlights to shake her hand."

Although she officially retired from show business in 1956, Josephine Baker has made special appearances to raise funds for the care of her international family. Her brother and sister also live at Les Milandes, her French chateau, and her mother spent her last years there.

HARRY BELAFONTE

Folk Singer-Actor

[1927-   ]

THE PHENOMENAL success of Harry Belafonte as a folk singer and actor was achieved in slightly less than five years. From a relatively unknown singer in 1951 at the Village Vanguard in New York City, he quickly became an outstanding entertainer in leading night clubs.

Born on March 1, 1927, in New York City, he was christened Harold George Belafonte, Jr., by his parents, Harold George and Melvene (Love) Belafonte. His father was a native of Martinique, French West Indies, where he had been a plantation owner, and his mother was born in Jamaica, British West Indies.

When Harry was eight years old, the family moved to his mother's home in Jamaica and stayed there for five years. Living was not easy in the British West Indies, so they returned to New York, where the father could find work to support his family.

Harry attended St. Thomas the Apostle parochial school in New York, and later spent two years at George Washington High School. His formal education ended in 1944 when he left school to enlist in the U.S. Navy, serving a period of

45

three years. Upon his return to civilian life, Harry obtained a job as maintenance worker for an apartment house. One of the tenants gave him a ticket, as a tip, to see *Home Is the Hunter*, an American Negro Theatre production. This was the first legitimate show Harry had seen, and it started him thinking about a career as an actor.

Since he had no training or experience as an actor, Belafonte enrolled at Erwin Piscator's Dramatic Workshop under the G.I. Bill, the vocational rehabilitation training and educational program set up by the government for anyone who had served in any branch of the Armed Services. Students could enroll in institutions of higher learning or, on the approval of their counselors, could train in business, technical, vocational, or trade schools. Harry took advantage of this program and studied at the Dramatic Workshop, but was unable to obtain an acting job, so he went to work in a New York garment factory.

He did not give up the idea of becoming an actor, however, and often dropped in at the Royal Roost, a Broadway Jazz Club. One day the owner heard Harry sing in a Dramatic Workshop production and gave him an audition. He was so pleased with the way Harry sang that he offered him a two-week engagement at $70 a week to perform in the Club. This two-week engagement was extended to twenty-six weeks and a salary increase to $200 a week as a result of his popularity.

For the next two years Harry spent his time singing in night clubs throughout the United States, his earnings totaling $350 a week. It was then that he was given a contract with Capitol Recording Company to make records of his songs. But Belafonte was not too happy, for he had hoped to combine his singing with an acting career. Since he was deeply interested in American folk music, he decided to put aside his desire to act for a while and seriously study folk music.

Harry spent many hours in the Library of Congress playing records, listening attentively to the way they were sung, and afterwards interpreting them in his own style. He was often accompanied on these trips by his friend, Millard Thomas, who later became his accompanist. Together they built a repertoire of old and modern folk ballads. Few folk singers have an accompanist, but Harry wanted one so that his hands could stay free for the dramatic treatment he gave the songs.

In 1951, Belafonte was signed for a two-week engagement to sing at the Village Vanguard in New York City, and remained for fourteen weeks. He then went to the Blue Angel for a sixteen-week stay. A talent scout from Metro-Goldwyn-Mayer heard Belafonte sing and invited him to Hollywood for a screen test. Harry was quite pleased, for now his real ambition was about to be realized! The screen test was favorable, and he was given the leading role in the film *Bright Road*, which was released in 1953. During the filming of the picture he fulfilled engagements at the Mocambo in Beverly Hills, California, and the Thunderbird in Las Vegas, Nevada.

Belafonte was then engaged to play the featured role in *John Murray Anderson's Almanac*, which opened on Broadway in December, 1953. His rendition of "Hold 'em Joe," the calypso number, and "Acorn in the Meadow" brought him recognition from the critics as a great performer and singer.

When Otto Preminger, the Hollywood producer, saw him in *Almanac*, he offered Harry the leading role of "Joe" in the CinemaScope version of the all-Negro musical *Carmen Jones*, but neither Harry nor his co-star, Dorothy Dandridge, sang in the production. Opera-trained voices were dubbed in. The *New York Tribune* commented in a review of the musical, "Harry Belafonte's 'Joe' is a clean-cut American youth, handsome and guileless." *Carmen Jones* was one of the few American films entered in the Annual Film Festival at Cannes, France, in 1955, and was highly commended.

For three months, Harry toured thirty-six states and made ninety-four one-night stands in *Three for Tonight*, a musical-drama-dance production, before it went to Broadway. While the show was on Broadway, he sang at the Starlight Roof of the Waldorf-Astoria Hotel, which was the top entertainment spot in New York City, and had engagements on the West Coast waiting for him when the show closed.

Early in 1955, Harry fulfilled these West Coast engagements, appearing at the Riviera in Las Vegas, Hotel Ambassador's Coconut Grove in Los Angeles, and the Fairmont Hotel in San Francisco. In October, 1955, when he returned to New York, Belafonte made the first of five appearances on the NBC-TV Colgate Variety Hour, a twenty-minute folklore feature. On November 6, he co-starred as a young prize fighter with Ethel Waters in *Winner by Decision*, a non-musical drama. On his second performance on the Colgate Variety Hour, November 20, 1955, during his engagement at the Palmer House in Chicago, *Variety Magazine* noted, "Belafonte took the Empire Room by storm." The crowds flocked there to see and hear him.

Jack Gould of the *New York Times* called Belafonte "the most compelling new artist of the TV year (1955)" and said that he "sang the folk songs and spirituals with an almost overwhelming intensity." Brooks Atkinson wrote in the *New*

York Herald Tribune, "Belafonte sings every song with the fierce conviction of an evangelist," and Walter Kerr of the same paper described Harry's interpretation of a variety of moods and said, "The evening was one of those rare occasions when a major entertainer unforgettably announces his existence."

Harry Belafonte has made many album recordings for RCA Victor. They include the famous "Matilda," "Hold 'em Joe," "Scarlet Ribbons," "Shenandoah," and his own composition, "Mark Twain." His income from recordings, night clubs, films, and the theatre is said to have amounted annually to more than $350,000.

Belafonte has been the recipient of many awards, including the Antoinette Perry Award for the best feature act in a musical, 1953; Donaldson Award for outstanding achievement in the theatre, 1953–54; Show Business Award for artistry and merit, 1954; U.S. Department of State Award, 1958, and in 1960, the TV Academy Award for the musical *Tonight with Belafonte*. He is the president of Belafonte Enterprises, Inc., a member of CORE (Congress on Racial Equality), American Guild Variety Artists, and the American Federation of Television and Radio Artists.

He was married on June 18, 1948, to Marguerita Byrd, a child psychology teacher, whom he met while in the Navy. They had two daughters, Adrienne and Shari, but this marriage did not last. On March 8, 1957, he married Julie Robinson, and they have two children, David and Gina.

Although Harry Belafonte has made a success of his talents as a folk singer and actor, he has one burning ambition, and that is to write plays dealing with American folklore. He hopes to begin writing in the not too distant future.

NAT "KING" COLE
Pianist-Singer-Actor
[1919-1965]

ONE OF AMERICA'S most popular recording artists and
pianist was Nat "King" Cole, whose husky-voiced singing of
many songs caused them to hit the million mark in record
sales.

Born in Florence, Alabama, on March 18, 1919, he was
christened Nathaniel Adams Coles. His father, Rev. Edward
James Coles, was a Baptist minister, the pastor of the True
Light Baptist Church, and his mother, Perlina Coles, was a
devout church worker who directed the choir in her husband's church. Nathaniel had three brothers and a sister, all
musically inclined, taught by their mother to sing in the choir
and play the piano.

The family left Alabama when Nathaniel was four years
old and moved to Chicago, Illinois. It was soon discovered
that Nat was a near-genius. At the age of five years, he was
able to play on the piano by ear any tune he heard. By the
time he was twelve years old, Nat was playing both the organ
and piano so well that he became the organist in his father's
church. "I played everything from Bach to Rachmaninoff for
six years," he said, and proudly stated that "my mother was

the only music teacher I ever had."

Before he was graduated from Wendell Phillips High School, Nat became a professional pianist, playing with a band called The Rogues of Rhythm, headed by his brother, Eddie. Their evening engagements kept him up very late, and he had to rise early each morning to attend his high school classes. Many of the one-night appearances netted him only a dollar.

It was while playing with The Rogues of Rhythm that Nat joined *Shuffle Along*, an all-Negro review. The band played with the show for six weeks. When his brother decided that it was time for them to leave the review, Nat chose to remain. *Shuffle Along* traveled westward, but it was not a success on the road, and when they reached California, it dissolved. This left Nat stranded in Los Angeles.

He managed to find work playing the piano in what he described as "every beer joint in Los Angeles," often receiving only four or five dollars for his night's work. In one of these parlors Nat was given his "royal" title. A barmaid in fun stuck a paper crown on his head and laughingly said, "Look! King Cole!" This nickname stuck with him permanently. He became a fine jazz pianist, but was destined to be a singer, also.

In 1938, one of the club owners suggested that Nat organize a group to entertain at his small establishment. Nat hired a guitarist, a bass violinist, a drummer, and with himself at the piano, it was to have been a quartet. But the drummer failed to show up, and the "Nat Cole Trio" was born. (He had dropped the "s" from his family name).

The Trio was not quite an overnight sensation, but there was something in their cool style that caught the attention of the saloon society set. They were an instrumental group which played jazz to the liking of their audience.

Nat "King" Cole became a single quite by chance. A patron where the Trio was playing one night requested that he sing "Sweet Lorraine," but Nat declined, saying, "There is no singer in this group." When the patron persisted, and the club manager insisted that he please the person, he sang the song. The crowd in the audience applauded and asked for an encore. From then on, "The King" began singing in his distinctive, soft, purring voice. Nat later remarked, "It was a long time before my own father was reconciled to my singing jazz, but he finally got used to it."

In 1943, he signed a contract with Capitol Records and recorded a song he had written, with a title taken from the memory of one of his father's sermons, "Straighten Up and Fly Right." It was a tune about a monkey and a buzzard's ride in the sky, and became a wartime hit. Other recordings which followed were "Sweet Lorraine," "It's Only a Paper Moon," "I'm Through with Love," and "Route 66."

During this time the King Cole Trio was rising to the top of the jazz combo lists, and Nat as pianist and Moore as guitarist were acclaimed the best instrumentalists in their respective fields.

In 1947, with his hit recording of "The Christmas Song," the fact that Nat "King" Cole was destined to become a great singer became abundantly clear to everyone. He was called a balladeer from then on. Many of his later recordings sold a million copies, including "Nature Boy," "Mona Lisa," "Too Young," "Rambling Rose," "Love Is a Many-Splendored Thing," and "Unforgettable." He began making appearances in cities throughout the United States, and in England and Australia, singing before large audiences.

53

Mr. Cole was the recipient of many awards and honors, among them The Esquire Award as Pianist and Singer, 1944–47. He made numerous appearances for charitable organizations, and was one of the best-loved entertainers in America. He was the first Negro star with a musical show on radio in 1948–49, sponsored by Wildroot Cream Oil.

Then television beckoned to him. At first he was one of the guests on many shows, then in 1956, he was the star of his own show. It was the first nationwide network television show to have a Negro star as host. The program ran one year, with smooth production, celebrity guests, critical acclaim, and good viewer rating. The main thing it did not have was national sponsors. In December, 1957, when the Nat King Cole Show went off the air, the reason given was that the fall network schedule failed to give the show prime time. But Nat remarked, "The ad agencies are afraid of the dark. They don't want to take any chances. I think the show can be sold if the agency men look at it from a money point of view rather than at the race issue."

Cole played in seven motion pictures, including *Blue Gardenia*, and was the star of *St. Louis Blues*, in which he portrayed the life of W. C. Handy, the composer. In 1964, he made his last motion picture, *Cat Ballou*.

He signed a contract with Las Vegas' Sands Hotel for one-half million dollars for each of three successive yearly appearances. His fame spread abroad, and while in South America, Nat turned his visit into a personal good-will trip by doing charity performances for homeless Brazilian children and flood victims.

Nat "King" Cole's total record sales ran to $25,000,000 for Capitol Records. His voice has been called "sirupy," "velvety," "silky," and "pussy-willow soft." Gene Grove of the *New York Post* wrote, "The voice issues still, as it has for 25 years, from a wide, wide mouth to caress a wide, wide world with rock-candy clarity, a two-octave range, and the husky timbre of a hum through a paper-covered comb. It has been observed that Nat Cole, with his precise enunciation, will make certain everyone in the house hears every word."

In his later years, "King" Cole turned his attention to his earlier love, that of the musical review. His first attempt in 1960 was a show called *I'm with You*, which never reached Broadway because of poor reviews in the Midwest after leaving the West Coast. But Nat did not let this stop him. He tried again with *Sights and Sounds*, which was issued in three yearly productions. This fine musical played in one hundred cities across the United States—night clubs, theatres, concert stages—and grossed an estimated million dollars in 1964.

With public acclaim for *Sights and Sounds*, Nat "King" Cole now stood at the pinnacle of success as a performer. He also was an astute businessman, owning three music publishing firms and the Kell-Cole Productions, which produced his musical shows.

In 1948, Nat married Maria Ellington, a singer with the Duke Ellington (no relation) band. He and his wife and their five children, Carol, Natalie, Kelly, and twins Casey and Timolin, lived in a spacious mansion in the Los Angeles exclusive Hancock Park area.

On December 8, 1964, Nat "King" Cole became ill and entered a hospital where it was learned he had cancer of the throat. He died on February 15, 1965.

SAMMY DAVIS, JR.

Dancer - Actor

[1925-   ]

SAMMY DAVIS, JR.'s whole life has been centered in the entertainment world. His first birthday was spent in a crib in the dressing room of the Hippodrome Theatre in New York City while his parents performed. He became a part of the family vaudeville act at the age of three years.

He was born on December 8, 1925, in New York City, the son of Sam and Elvira (Sanchez) Davis. His mother and father were dancers, members of the Will Mastin vaudeville act called "Holiday in Dixieland," which was very popular during the 1920's. His mother stayed with the act until Sammy was two years old, leaving the cast when his little sister, Ramona, was born.

Sammy grew up on the road as the Will Mastin act, headed by Will Mastin, an adopted uncle, traveled from city to city. They played in small towns and cities wherever they could get an engagement in vaudeville shows or cabarets. The troupe was often stranded and broke, but always managed to get to the next engagement.

At a theatre in Michigan, the late Bill "Bojangles" Robinson saw the act and was so impressed with Sammy's ability he asked Mr. Mastin to bring the boy to him. For countless hours, Sammy was shown the skill and showmanship that had made "Bojangles" a success. Within a year Sammy, in Robinson's opinion, had become a perfectionist with his dance steps.

In 1946, Will Mastin cut the members of his act from seven to five and then to three: himself, Sammy Davis, Sr., and Sammy Davis, Jr. Thereafter, the Will Mastin Trio, as they were then billed, began to attract the top night clubs of the country, with Sammy, Jr., featured in solo dances and impersonations. They were booked into Slapsie Maxie's in Hollywood and appeared as the opening act, which is where most unknown performers are placed. But their reception was so overwhelming that they were signed for a return engagement as headliners.

In September, 1947, at a Los Angeles theatre, the Trio appeared on the same bill with Mickey Rooney for a two-week stay, and remained for six months. They later played the Palace Theatre in Columbus, Ohio, where the Trio was headlined with Jimmy Dorsey, and at the Capitol Theatre in New York City with Frank Sinatra, and in Los Angeles with Bob Hope. In 1950, the Will Mastin Trio was on the same bill with Jack Benny, Dennis Day, and other top names in the entertainment world. When the act was engaged to play at Ciro's in Hollywood, Sammy, Jr., was earning $300 a week, which seemed like a fortune to him.

In the fall of 1953, ABC-TV made a pilot film called *Three's Company*, with an interracial setting, and Sammy, Jr., was asked to play a part in the film. It was to have been a series, but the project was abandoned after a year.

Sammy made his debut at New York's Copacabana in 1954, and received such enthusiastic press notices that Decca Records gave him a contract. He made two albums, each with eleven titles, "Starring Sammy Davis, Jr.," in which he featured his impersonations of Martin and Lewis, Jimmy Durante, Frank Sinatra, Johnny Ray, Arthur Godfrey, Bing Crosby, and many other celebrities.

He was fulfilling an engagement at the Last Frontier in Las Vegas, on November 19, 1954, when Sammy was called to a recording session in Hollywood. While driving there, he collided with another automobile and was taken to a hospital in San Bernardino, critically injured. Three days later his left eye had to be removed. When he was fully recovered, he again made appearances in night clubs and theatres. He wore a patch over his eye after the accident, and one day Humphrey Bogart said to him, "You think you're pretty jazzy with that Glen plaid eye patch, but it's a big mistake. Take it off!" And Sammy took it off and has used a glass eye ever since.

On February 15, 1955, Sammy Davis, Jr., entertained at Copa City, in Miami Beach, Florida, with his extensive repertoire, dancing, singing, and giving impersonations, and received a standing ovation. When he appeared at the Copacabana in New York City on March 17, 1955, Frank Quinn of the *New York Mirror* commented on his "remarkable showmanship" and said that the act was "polished to perfection" as he did imitations of Frankie Laine, Tony Bennett, Vaughn Monroe, and Billy Daniels.

During 1956–57, Sammy was the star of the Broadway musical hit, *Mr. Wonderful*. In his review of the opening night, March 26, 1956, Brooks Atkinson of the *New York Times* wrote, "It was a spectacular, noisy endorsement of mediocrity that came alive when Sammy rocks and rolls, taps and does imitations." All the critics agreed that Sammy was "one of the foremost exponents of a kind of vocal delivery that takes a new step toward pandemonium in popular music; a tap dancer of formidable agility, and a pleasantly accomplished mimic." Radio disc jockeys began putting Sammy on the air, playing songs from the show which included the title song, "Mr. Wonderful," "Too Close for Comfort," "Without You," and others. Sammy was chosen to star in the film version of the Broadway hit.

He made TV appearances on Ed Sullivan's "Toast of the Town," the Milton Berle Show, and the Colgate Comedy Hour, which added to his popularity. In March, 1957, he was signed by Frank Sinatra to co-star in the musical comedy movie, *The Jazz Train*, a United Artists release. He had previously relinquished a movie contract with Metro-Goldwyn-Mayer for *St. Louis Woman* in order to star in the Broadway musical, *Mr. Wonderful*.

For three years, beginning in 1959, Sammy Davis, Jr., played important roles in the film versions of *Anna Lucasta* and *Porgy and Bess*, and the movies *Ocean's 11*, *Convicts Four*, and *Johnny Cool*. He became the star of another Broadway hit, *Golden Boy*, in 1964, in which he became the highest-paid Broadway performer in history, receiving $10,000 a week plus fringe benefits. In the play, Sammy sang ten songs, did four dances, and turned from comedy to a delicate love scene, and ended with a grueling prize fight.

While he was playing in *Golden Boy* on Broadway, Sammy made a film which was shot in New York named *A Man Called Adam* with Frank Sinatra, Jr., as his co-star. During this time, in the fall of 1965, he was asked by the National Broadcasting Company to be the star of his own television show. Sammy worked hard and tireless to make his TV première outstanding. In addition to this, he fulfilled numerous requests for personal appearances and benefit shows, including The American Cancer Society, United Jewish Appeal, The Medical Committee for Human Rights, NAACP, CORE, and SNCC.

Because of previous contracts, Sammy Davis, Jr., had to be absent from his television variety show for four weeks after its première. The first show, in January, 1966, with Sammy as star and host, received very high ratings. One critic said, "The host and star of the show can dance rings around any other host. He can sing with the best. He is more graceful, more energetic, and a much better impressionist than any other host on any other variety show." During his absence from the show, the ratings went down, but upon his return, the Sammy Davis TV Hour, with top entertainers and Sammy himself, a master showman, was rated as one of the best productions on the air. But it only lasted six weeks after Sammy's return, and he did the last show entirely alone, without the help of any guest stars.

No personality in show business is more honored than Sammy Davis, Jr. He thrives on performing because it is what he knows best. Rarely has an artist crowded more work and activity into a career than Sammy. He says, "I'm not sure what makes me move so compulsively toward a higher goal, but I feel that life is only meaningful if one makes things happen."

He has so much energy that it seems to be inexhaustible. "He keeps up his terrific pace because of his will to succeed," says his executive secretary, Shirley Rhodes. He is the head of Sammy Davis Enterprises, which has lavish offices that occupy an entire floor of a large building on 56th Street in Manhattan, New York. Sammy is a very ambitious young man and is not content to be a Broadway and television star, but wants to own the whole building in which his offices are located. He says his greatest ambition is "to produce four movies and to hire Kirk Douglas, John Wayne, and Frank Sinatra."

On November 13, 1960, Sammy married actress Mai Britt, and they now have three children. When in California, they live in a luxurious fifteen-room mansion in Hollywood Hills; and they rent a $1,000-a-month duplex apartment in New York City.

By any standards, Sammy Davis, Jr. is a super-star, and has now received the ultimate acclaim of stardom with the publication of his autobiography, *Yes, I Can*. The story was dictated to a pair of friends, Jane and Burt Boyar, and told with some humor and a little sentimentality of his rise to fame and the limits of his success. Sammy refuses to be stopped by racial barriers. "I'm aware of the fact that if I break down a barrier, others will benefit," he says. "I'm not going to let anybody tell me I can't do this or that, because I'm going to do it in show business if I prepare myself for it."

"DUKE" ELLINGTON
Pianist - Composer - Band Leader
[1899–   ]

Edward Kennedy Ellington was born April 29, 1899, in Washington, D.C. His father, J. E. Ellington, was a blueprint tracer in the Navy yard, and his mother, Daisy, was a housewife who took a great deal of interest in her son. When Edward was seven years old, his mother arranged for him to start taking piano lessons after school. "Though I liked music, I never got on with practicing lessons," he confesses. "Before I knew it, I would be fashioning a new melody and accompaniment instead of following the score."

Edward had not planned to be a composer or musician. He had thought he wanted to be a commercial artist, so he studied painting in his early teens, and during his last year in high school he won a scholarship for the Pratt Institute of Fine Arts in Brooklyn. He loved sports, and baseball took up almost as much of his time as painting. He was a good center fielder, and sometimes played second base when called upon to change his position on the field. But he continued to study the piano. His scholastic record in high school was not very good, for sometimes in classes, Edward and the boys around him would set up such a racket, beating out ragtime rhythms

63

on their desks, the teacher would have to call for order. It was in high school that he acquired the nickname "Duke" because of his immaculate appearance.

"Duke" started working in an ice cream parlor and poolroom called the Poodle Dog after school, where there was a piano on which he was often called to play. This helped him change his mind about being an artist, and made him consider a career as a musician.

When he was seventeen, the leader of a society band offered "Duke" a place in his band if by evening he could play "Siren Song." He spent all day learning the tune, but when he arrived on the job, "Duke" found that he would have to know about correct chords. On the spur of the moment, he decided to use a trick—that of throwing his hands away from the piano. "Before I knew what was happening, the kids around the bandstand were screaming and clapping for more. In two minutes, my flashy hands had earned me a reputation, and after that I was all set," Duke recalls.

Fascinated by ragtime music, Ellington studied the technique of J. P. Johnson and other great exponents of this style. He wrote his first full composition, "Soda Fountain Rag," at the age of seventeen, which showed that he had real musical talent. So, after serving a short time as pianist with the band of Louis Thomas, he organized his own band, who called themselves The Washingtonians, and sometimes The Wildcats, and many of these men are still with "Duke."

In 1918, he decided to go to New York to try out his new band, but they went broke and had to return to Washington. "Duke" was so discouraged he was considering quitting the band business, when Fats Waller wired him to return to New York. In 1923 he and his five-piece band were hired by the

Kentucky Club, where many celebrities came. One of the music publishers, Irving Mills, almost immediately placed Ellington under contract and helped him to enlarge his band to twelve pieces. He was particularly interested in "Duke" as a composer and in making his orchestra available for recordings.

"Duke" and his orchestra made a surprising number of recordings, including many transcriptions for radio. Of twenty-eight records given top rating in *Swing* during 1940, seventeen were Ellington's. The band was already broadcasting over WHN every day, when the Columbia Broadcasting System put them on the air. At this time the orchestra began to appear on the leading theatre stages. They played in Florenz Ziegfeld's *Show Girl* and were featured in several films, *Check and Double Check* with Amos 'n' Andy, "She Got Her Man" with Mae West, and Earl Carroll's *Murder at the Vanities*.

In 1927, "Duke" and his band opened at the Cotton Club, the number-one showplace for jazz bands in New York. He made a record stay at the Club, and in 1933 they toured Europe. They were such a hit, the orchestra again toured Europe in 1939, playing twenty-eight concerts in France, Holland, Norway, Denmark, and Sweden. In Paris, Duke played twice to a full house at the bomb-proof underground Theatre National de Chillot, doing some of his best-known numbers, "Mood Indigo," "Rocking in Rhythm," "Solitude," "Harmony in Harlem," and his own arrangement of Rachmaninoff's "Prelude in C Sharp Minor."

Through his recordings and his tours, "Duke" is almost as well known in Europe as in the United States. During the orchestra's first European tour in 1933, one of his most enthusiastic listeners was the Duke of Windsor, then Prince of Wales, who had one of the best collections of Ellington records in Europe.

In 1943, at his annual Carnegie Hall concert, "Duke" premiered an original forty-minute suite, "Black, Brown and Beige," a tone parallel to the history of the American Negro, which drew its inspiration from spirituals, chain gang songs, field hollers, blues, and all the music the Negro had given to America.

Among other long, serious works, in which the elements of jazz are fused into concert hall compositions, were "New World A-coming," "Liberian Suite," and "Tattooed Bride." Ellington has written numerous musical scores, including "Jump for Joy," and "Beggar's Holiday." He was commissioned by the NBC Symphony Orchestra, under the direction of Arturo Toscanini, to produce "Harlem," and conducted that orchestra in its debut.

"Duke" Ellington has shown that jazz compositions may be skillful portraits—of a mood, of a period, of a man. His first, "Soda Fountain Rag" belongs to the days of "jerking" sodas at the Poodle Dog; "Bojangles" creates Bill Robinson for the listener; "Sophisticated Lady" was inspired by a schoolteacher in Washington, D.C. All of them have deep meaning for him. He received the $2,500 ASCAP Prize for "Solitude" in 1934.

Although it is "jazz" or "swing" with which "Duke" is associated, his music differs from that of any other composer or conductor whose name is associated with the word. Ellington composes his own tunes, contributes the harmony, makes his own arrangements, and, as a pianist-composer-conductor, interprets the music. He controls the men in his orchestra from the piano with movements of his head, shoulders, elbows, as well as his hands. He is called "The Aristocrat of Swing," "The King of Swing," and "The King of Jazz."

For over forty years, Ellington has produced a ceaseless flow of high-quality modern music. His contribution to American musical literature is unparalleled. He has managed to blend the technique of the classics with the inspiration of America's musical heritage, and at the same time, to give them both a uniquely Ellington twist. "Duke" feels that the word "jazz" is a misnomer. "I feel we all would have been better off if we had started out calling it Negro music. We Negroes are responsible for more than ninety-nine percent of it anyway," he says.

"Duke" Ellington is first in the hearts of the world as a composer, pianist, and band leader. He has a long string of "firsts" to his credit. He made a first appearance with the Boston Pops Orchestra and the first of his many RCA Victor albums appeared on the Red Seal label. Recorded live at the successful Boston Pops Pension Fund Concert at Tanglewood, Massachusetts, the album is appropriately titled "The Duke at Tanglewood." Included in the diamond-studded classic are the well-known "Caravan," "Mood Indigo," "Sophisticated Lady," "Solitude," "Do Nothing 'Til you Hear from Me," "I'm Beginning to See the Light," and "Satin Doll."

Mr. Ellington was married in 1918 to Edna Thompson, his high school sweetheart, and they have one son, Mercer, who studied at the Juilliard School of Music in New York, and now has a band of his own.

In 1965, at the age of sixty-six, the jazz musician, composer, and band leader, "Duke" Ellington, was recommended by the Music Jury of the Advisory Board for the Pulitzer Prizes for a special citation for long-term achievement. Ellington commented on his rejection for the award with philosophical acceptance. He stated, "Fate's being kind to me. Fate doesn't want me to be too famous too young."

LENA HORNE
Singer--Movie Star
[1917–   ]

THE BEAUTIFUL face of a lovely woman was seen on the motion picture screens of America in *Panama Hattie;* it was the first time a Negro singer had appeared with white actors as a featured star in a motion picture. Lena Horne's beauty, personality, and poise made her the most photographed Negro in the world.

She was born in Brooklyn, New York, on June 30, 1917. Her parents, Edwin F. and Edna (Scotchron) Horne, were divorced when Lena was three years old. She lived in a house on Chauncey Street with her grandparents until she was six or seven years of age. Lena remembers it had an iron fence around it which separated the house from the sidewalk.

Her childhood was not a very happy one. She was nearly always with adults, as her association with children was limited to a few in the neighborhood who met with her grandmother's approval. Sometimes Lena would put on some of her mother's or grandmother's clothes and play "dress-up." If the weather was good, she would go out in the back yard and play under the cherry tree by herself.

Lena's mother was an actress with the old Lafayette Players, one of the most successful Negro theatrical groups at that time. She took Lena with her on many of her tours, from city to city, but decided that she was not able to take proper care of her only child. So Lena went to live with distant relatives and friends of the family, always returning to the home of her grandparents in Brooklyn for brief periods of time.

She says, "I find it almost impossible to remember the sequence of the houses in which I lived and the people who took care of me. Nor is it possible to remember exactly how long I stayed in one particular place." She perhaps lived in Fort Valley, Georgia, longer than any other place, for she attended a little Rosenwald-endowed school across the street from Fort Valley High and Industrial School, where her Uncle Frank was dean. She lived in the dormitory with older girls, but was too young to attend the high school.

At sixteen, Lena was back in New York attending Girls High School in Brooklyn, when she decided to leave school and get a job. Through her mother's connections, she obtained a place in the chorus line at the famous Cotton Club in Harlem, in the show *Stormy Weather*, appearing with Adelaide Hall, Cab Calloway, and the Nicholas brothers. For two years, Lena danced in the reviews at the Club and sang occasional solos. Soon she was being featured in the show as a singer and dancer with Avon Long, the star.

Lena had little experience as a singer, but her technique attracted the attention of the actor, Flournoy Miller, who recommended her to Noble Sissle; and in February, 1936, she went on a road tour with the Noble Sissle Band. They were booked to play at a dance hall called the Moonlight Gardens in Cincinnati, when Noble Sissle was hospitalized because of an accident. He asked Lena to direct the band. At first she refused, but upon his insistence, she agreed. So, on opening night, Lena directed the band in addition to singing. Newspapers, the next day, reported that there was a good band at the Moonlight Gardens, "The Noble Sissle Orchestra, directed by Lena Horne." It was a "first" for the band as well as Lena's first attempt at directing, for no other Negro band had ever played at the Moonlight Gardens.

In Pittsburgh, she met a young printer, Louis Jones, and shortly thereafter they were married. Two children were born, Gail (1938) and Edwin (1940). Lena stayed with the Noble Sissle Band as the featured soloist for three years. During that time she gained a great deal of experience and some small fame as a singer. As a result she was offered a role in Lew Leslie's *Blackbirds of 1939*, a yearly production, but this edition of the review unfortunately closed after only nine performances. In addition to this, her marriage was not working out well, and she finally was divorced.

In 1940, a friend told Lena that Charlie Barnett was looking for a woman vocalist for his band, and she applied. She was instantly hired and did the show that same evening, thus becoming the first Negro girl to be featured with a white dance band. In March, 1941, Miss Horne opened at the Cafe Society Downtown in New York City and was such a success that three weeks later, Barney Josephson, the owner, sponsored her in a concert at Carnegie Hall. She won the hearts of her audience with her style of presenting songs as well as her charm and beauty.

Lena received an invitation to sing at Hollywood's Little Troc Cabaret in February, 1942, and at the Mocambo in July. She was well received at both places, and a *New York Times* reporter wrote of her in his column, "She came on without an introduction and started to sing without even announcing her number. She sang 'The Man I Love' and 'Stormy Weather,' and the crowd went wild and clapped for more."

It was during her engagement at the Cafe Society Downtown that she was seen by a film executive, and before the end of her engagement, Metro-Goldwyn-Mayer had signed her to motion pictures.

Lena was given a small part in *Panama Hattie* in 1942, and impressed her audiences with her golden beauty and her acting ability. It was the first role in which no stereotype was displayed. She was a beautiful actress playing her part in the movie along with Ann Sothern and the others. Later, she played the part of Georgia Brown in the film version of *Cabin in the Sky*. Her acting was so satisfactory that she was given a seven-year contract with Metro-Goldwyn-Mayer.

Other movies in which she starred or had an important role include *Stormy Weather* (1943), *As Thousands Cheer* (1943), *Swing River* (1944), *Broadway Rhythm* (1944), and *Two Girls and a Sailor* (1944). She has been received enthusiastically with considerable mention of her "luscious, dark glamor." Elsa Maxwell once said, "Lena has a voice, a most clear, distinctive and articulate voice. Opinions may differ, but it is there."

In *Leader Magazine*, October 11, 1947, James Mason included Lena Horne in his list of the six best actresses in Hollywood. She was known for her downright and courageous attitude toward Hollywood's attempts at discrimination, and for her refusal to play in stage or screen roles which did not reflect credit on the Negro race as a whole. Lena had said, "All we ask of the motion-picture industry is that the Negro be portrayed as a normal person; as a voter at the polls;

as an elected official; as a civil service worker."

One of her most satisfying experiences, Lena declares, was when she launched the Liberty Ship *George Washington Carver*, named after the world-famous scientist, for whom she has long had an intense admiration.

In December, 1964, WNEW-TV presented a fitting tribute to the singer. It was a musical hour entitled "Lena," with the music directed by her husband, Lennie Hayton, whom she married in 1947 in Paris, France. The program presented Lena in all of the standard and well-loved songs which have become identified with her stunning talent.

"I may be admired as an artist," she has said, "but I wouldn't say that I'm a performer who necessarily evokes a loving reaction from the audience. I have this sense of privacy. I'm giving tremendously but I don't ask the audience to. I don't want them to invade beyond a certain point, and I don't want to impose any attitudes on them. I think, sometimes, it must be fun to have this kind of hold on an audience, though, to be funny or sad or just appealing." For Lena, the need to be creative takes emphatic precedence over a yearning for unremittent audience approval.

Lena Horne has made many appearances on television shows, and sings her songs with all her heart. During these years, she was at work on her autobiography, which was published by Doubleday in 1965 under the title *Lena*.

EARTHA KITT

Singer - Actress

[1928–   ]

WILLIAM KITT was a sharecropper on a small farm in the town of North, South Carolina. On January 26, 1928, the day his daughter was born, he had his first good harvest in many years. To thank the earth, he named the newborn baby "Eartha." Another girl was born a little more than a year later, named Anna Pearl, after her mother. Mr. Kitt disappeared soon afterward and was not seen again. He was later reported dead.

Eartha's mother, Anna Mae (Riley) Kitt, tried to keep the little farm going after her husband's disappearance, but she was not well, and the work was too hard for her. Within a few years she died, leaving eight-year-old Eartha and her little sister to drift from neighbor to neighbor for a while. Mrs. Kitt's sister, Mamie Lue Riley, finally sent for the two little girls to come and live with her in New York City.

Mrs. Riley and her husband lived in a Puerto Rican-Italian section of New York, and Eartha soon picked up the languages of her little playmates. She attended the public school in the neighborhood and became quite enthusiastic about sports, playing baseball and excelling at pole vaulting.

75

Left alone much of the time after school, since her aunt and uncle both had to work, Eartha created a world of fantasy which dominated her love for music and dancing. She made up little songs and did rhythmic steps in time to the tune she was humming. She was called upon to perform at school affairs when her aptitude in this art became known, and won several prizes for her interpretative dances. Eartha went to the Salem Methodist Church and, because of her love for music, began singing in the choir.

Eartha left school at the age of fourteen and went to work in a Brooklyn factory to help supplement the earnings of her aunt and supply the needed clothing for her sister to continue school. But she used some of the money to take piano lessons, and soon after her sixteenth birthday, a friend arranged an audition for her with Katherine Dunham, the well-known dance instructor. This resulted in a scholarship, and Miss Kitt joined the Katherine Dunham Dance Troupe.

Her natural instinct for and enjoyment of dancing made her an apt pupil, and in 1947 she was selected to go on a tour of the United States, Mexico, and South America with the Troupe. When it was discovered that she could sing, she was taught Haitian, African, and Cuban songs and soon became the vocalist for the Troupe.

In 1948, the Dunham Dance Troupe went to Europe, and Eartha sang and danced at the Prince of Wales Theatre in London before an audience which included the Royal family. They went on to Paris and other European countries. She was greeted with enthusiasm at Kervansaray in Istanbul, where her dazzling costumes and her ability to sing in many languages impressed her night club audience.

When the Dance Troupe returned to the United States,

Eartha decided to stay abroad. She went back to Paris, where she got an engagement singing at Carroll's, a smart night club, and was an instant success. Her successful engagement was interrupted in 1951 when her Aunt Mamie, who took her in as a child, died. Eartha quickly flew to New York for the funeral.

Upon her return to Paris, Orson Welles asked Eartha to play Helen of Troy in *Faust*, and she accepted. With only two days to learn the part, her performance drew praise from the critics on opening night. In an interview with Ted Poston of the *New York Post*, Miss Kitt said, "I learned so much from Orson Welles just by keeping my mouth shut and listening. He gave me my first chance at a legitimate stage role." The Parisian newspaper *France-Soir* gave Eartha second place in its annual award for "the greatest acting achievement of the year" (1951) for her performance. The play was later shortened to concert form and made a brief tour through Germany and Belgium.

After "*Faust*" closed, Eartha Kitt starred in two French films, and was about to begin another when Monte Proser of "La Vie en Rose" invited her to sing at his New York night club. Her return to the entertainment world in the United States was not a happy occasion, as her debut at the Club was not well received. But she established her first American success in 1952 at Max Gordon's Village Vanguard, where she stayed for twenty-five weeks, filling the club to capacity, singing "C'est Si Bon" and other sophisticated European songs.

Producer Leonard Sillman saw her at the Village Vanguard, and gave her a part in his review, *New Faces of 1952*. Eartha was a sensation with her "combustible" singing of the song "Monotonous," and when Twentieth Century Fox produced the review in CinemaScope on the screen, she sang several songs especially composed for her as well as others associated with her.

While in Hollywood with Twentieth Century Fox, Eartha fulfilled an engagement at the Mocambo in November, 1953, and broke a thirteen-year attendance record. She gave a command performance for the King and Queen of Greece during that same month.

Miss Kitt has appeared in many motion pictures, and was the star in *Accused*, 1957; *Anna Lucasta*, 1958; *The Mark of the Hawk*; and *St. Louis Blues*, with Nat "King" Cole. She sang on several television shows, including the Colgate Comedy Hour, Your Show of Shows, The Toast of the Town. Edward R. Murrow's Person to Person program showed Eartha at home in her Riverside Drive penthouse on September 11, 1954.

From $250 a week at the Village Vanguard in 1952, Miss Kitt's night club earnings increased to $10,000 weekly in 1954, when she appeared at El Rancho in Las Vegas. Her personality and ability to sing with feeling made her famous. She was praised highly for her calypso number "Somebody Bad Stole de Wedding Bell" and "Santa, Baby."

Leonard Sillman, remembering her achievement in his *New Faces of 1952*, chose her for the leading role in his stage play *Mrs. Patterson*, which opened on December 1, 1954, at the National Theatre in New York. Walter Kerr of the *New York Herald* called her an "enchanting gamin" in her portrayal of Teddy Hicks, the fifteen-year-old daughter of a Kentucky laundress. The play, which starred the actress-singer in her first dramatic role on Broadway, was described as "salty" and "earthy," while Miss Kitt was described as "impressively feline," "sultry," "sloe-eyed," and with a "haunting voice."

Eartha remarked that in preparing for the part she studied the actions of her pet cats "Tex" and "Finnegan," because "cats respond very much the same way as children." William Hawkins wrote in his review of the play for the *New York World-Telegram and Sun*, "Nobody who goes to see *Mrs. Patterson* will doubt that Eartha Kitt is destined to be one of the major figures of our theatre." The play closed on February 26, 1955, after 101 performances.

In June, 1960, Eartha was married to William O. McDonald, and they have a daughter, Kitt McDonald, who travels with Eartha on her singing engagements. Remembering her own lonesome childhood, with both her parents gone, she says, "I want to spend as much time with Kitt as I possibly can. I like to feed her and dress her and tuck her in bed at night. I want her to feel loved and wanted."

Eartha Kitt rose from abject poverty to become a famous night club singer and demonstrated her talent as a dramatic actress on Broadway. People have commented on her capacity for hard work and painstaking precision. She speaks six languages fluently and reads about four books a week. She is still active in sports, and plays tennis and golf whenever possible.

Miss Kitt wrote her own autobiography which was published in 1958, called *Thursday's Child*. She gave it this title because she was born on Thursday, and remembered the nursery rhyme,

> "Monday's child is fair of face,
> Tuesday's child is full of grace,
> Wednesday's child is full of woe,

Thursday's child has far to go,
Friday's child is loving and giving,
Saturday's child must work for a living;
But the child who is born on the Sabbath day
Is bonnie and blithe and good and gay."

SIDNEY POITIER

Actor - Academy Award Winner

[1924-   ]

REGINALD and Evelyn (Outten) Poitier were tomato farmers on Cat Island in the Bahama Islands. Once or twice a year they went to Florida in a small sailboat to sell their tomatoes. It was on one of these trips, February 20, 1924, that their youngest child, Sidney, was born, in Miami, Florida. He was the eighth child of his parents, and the only one born in the United States. When Sidney was old enough, his parents returned with him to Cat Island.

Sidney's childhood on the Island was happy and uncomplicated. With the sea as a backyard, the sunny days were spent largely in building rafts and in fishing. He says, "I used to stand on shore and watch ships until they disappeared. I would then dream of the far-away places they would go to and wonder if I would ever be able to travel." The family stayed on Cat Island until the tomato farm began to fail.

When Sidney was eleven years old, they moved to Nassau and for the first time in his life he saw automobiles, electric lights, and had his first ice cream cone. But living in Nassau was not much better than on Cat Island for the Poitiers. They lived in a succession of two-room wooden shacks with leaking

81

roofs, outdoor kitchens, and no modern facilities.

In Nassau, Sidney began going to school at Western Senior High School and Governor's High School. He had to quit after two years, as his father's health was failing, and Sidney went to work to help supplement the family income. He took a job as a water-boy with an island construction concern, and by the time he was thirteen years old, he was a laborer, swinging a pick and working with a shovel.

With the few pennies he had for himself from his weekly salary, he would go to the movies with his friends. Some of these boys were of bad character, and once they stole corn from a farmer, and Sidney's father had to pay a fine. On another occasion he and the other boys stole a bicycle and his father tried hard and succeeded in keeping Sidney from going to a reform school. It was then that Mr. Poitier decided to send Sidney to the United States to live with an older brother in Miami, Florida.

Sidney had a West Indian accent, which was a handicap because he could hardly make himself understood, but he was able to obtain a job as messenger boy for a drugstore. There, in Florida, Sidney, as a teen-ager, first became conscious of the color line. He recalls, "My life became full of frustration and confusion, because I found I could not trust adults."

He did not like Miami, and so at the age of sixteen, Sidney decided to go to New York. He had very little money, and had to hitch-hike and ride in the box cars of trains, until he reached New York's Harlem. When he arrived there, he had only $1.50 in his pocket.

Poitier found work as a dishwasher and slept on the roof across from the Capitol Theatre in warm weather. When the weather became too cold for this, he rented a cheap room in one of the hotels. He later worked as dockhand, longshore-man, short-order cook, and waiter. When the attack was made on Pearl Harbor, Sidney enlisted in the U.S. Army, was trained as a physiotherapist with a medical detachment, and was assigned to the Military Psychopathic Ward in a Long Island hospital. He was discharged in 1945.

Sidney went back to New York after his discharge from the Army, and when he read in the newspaper that the American Negro Theatre was looking for actors, he applied. His audition was not very favorable, and the director, Frederick O'Neal, said that he did not feel Sidney had the required talents to become an actor.

This, however, made Poitier more determined than ever to make good at acting, for he had decided that this was what he wanted to do. He bought a small radio and spent as much time as he possibly could listening to cultivated voices and improving his own speech by repeating words and phrases he heard on the radio, trying to eliminate his Bahamian accent. He studied hard, and after six months, when he again went to the Theatre, Mr. O'Neal agreed to give him acting lessons in exchange for backstage chores.

Sidney became a member of the Actors' Group, and soon advanced enough to act out small parts in some of the plays. He later alternated with Harry Belafonte in the leading role of *Days of Our Youth*, and played the butler in *Striver's Road*.

In 1946, he got his first big break when a Broadway director, who was casting an all-Negro version of the Greek play *Lysistrata*, saw him in a student production and signed him to a twelve-line part. The production ran only four days, but he impressed all who saw him and was signed for an understudy role in a company of *Anna Lucasta* that was going on a nation-wide tour. Before the end of the tour, Sidney was given the leading role.

For the next three years he played many roles in cities from coast to coast. In 1949, Sidney took a screen test which proved to be favorable. He made his first film appearance in an Army Signal Corps Documentary called *From Whom Cometh My Help,* and in 1950 made his Hollywood film debut in Twentieth Century Fox's *No Way Out,* portraying the role of a young doctor.

His performance in this film caused Howard Barnes of the *New York Herald Tribune* to comment, "Poitier is particularly good as the doctor who had to hurdle both his color and the exacting demands of his profession." He then played the part of a young priest in *Cry the Beloved Country,* and in 1955 had the leading part in *Blackboard Jungle,* a movie dealing with juvenile delinquency in the New York schools. Sidney played the part of a gifted student whose rude behavior creates havoc in every classroom. Later he directs his energies toward constructive ends with the help of a teacher who believes in him.

Other movies in which he starred were *Edge of the City, Band of Angels,* and *Something of Value.* In 1958, he skyrocketed to fame for his outstanding performance in *The Defiant Ones.* In this picture, he is one of a pair of convicts, the other a white man, who escape from a prison van, but are chained together. Although they hate each other at first, they learn to respect one another eventually. The movie is based on the belief that brotherhood and the mutual respect of man for man is a desirable goal, regardless of race or color. For his superb acting in *The Defiant Ones* Sidney was nominated for

84

an Academy Award, and received the Silver Bear Award at the Berlin Film Festival of 1958. The film also won the New York Film Critics' Award and was named to six of the "best ten movies" list.

In spite of the limited casting opportunities the Hollywood film industry offers Negro actors, Sidney became the first of his race to be nominated as the best actor by the Academy of Motion Picture Arts and Sciences for his performance in *The Defiant Ones*. Sidney said he believed the film had universal appeal, because "whether we like it or not, we are chained together, and if one of us drowns, the other is going down, too."

Poitier has successfully appeared in many other motion pictures, among them *All the Young Men, Point Blank, Porgy and Bess, The Bedford Incident*, and *The Long Ships*. In 1959, Sidney appeared on Broadway, starring in Lorraine Hansberry's drama, *A Raisin in the Sun*. This play depicts a Negro family living in Chicago who are trying to cross the boundary line that separates lower-class status from the middle class. Poitier plays the part of the high-strung son who has to make a big decision concerning his desire for material things, or whether to stand firm for freedom and dignity.

Sidney himself has said, "All that matters to me is what I get out of the part. I don't mean money; what I want is the kind of role that makes me feel worth-while. I will work anywhere—movies, theatre, and TV, provided the material has texture, quality—something good to say about life."

It was for his portrayal of a footloose Baptist handyman who helped some nuns to build a church in *Lilies of the Field* that Sidney Poitier became the first of his race to win filmdom's top acting award, the "Oscar," in 1964. In accepting the award, Poitier said, "Because it is a long journey to this moment, I am naturally indebted to countless numbers of people, principal among them are Ralph Nelson (director of the film) and the members of the Academy."

In 1965, Sidney starred in *A Patch of Blue*, in which he befriended a young white blind girl. This won him wide acclaim. Speaking of his formula for success, Poitier stated, "You must have a natural gift, and be willing to pay the price. The price is hard work, stubbornness, toughness and tenacity."

Everyone who has ever worked with him both likes and admires him as a man and as an actor. Sidney would have been called a credit to his race at an earlier time in history, but since his race is the human race, Poitier is merely a very good actor who has made a significant break-through. He says, "It leaves me feeling accomplished in a humble way, if that's possible. I do hope there will be some benefit for other Negro actors, but I don't fool myself into thinking that the effect will be vast. I'm an average Joe Blow Negro, but I'm out there wailing for us all. I'll never be able to function as freely as a Marlon Brando, or a Burt Lancaster, or a Paul Newman, but on the other side, I've had a kind of variety imposed on me that the others haven't. I've been able to work on material with more substance. Almost everything I've done has been controversial."

Sidney Poitier married Juanita Hardy, formerly a dancer, on April 29, 1950, and they have four daughters. He has a twelve-room home in Mt. Vernon, New York, where the family holds open house every Saturday and Sunday for their friends and neighbors. His parents now live in Nassau in a house Sidney had built for them.

LEONTYNE PRICE
Metropolitan Opera Singer
[1927–   ]

THE ONE AMBITION of Leontyne Price was to sing at the Metropolitan Opera in New York. This dream of the golden-voiced soprano from Mississippi came true on January 27, 1961, when she sang Leonora in *Il Trovatore* and was received with glowing reception from critics and opera lovers.

Mary Leontine Price was born February 10, 1927, in Laurel, Mississippi, one of two children of James Anthony and Kate (Baker) Price. Her father worked as a carpenter in a sawmill and her mother served as nurse or midwife in the community where they lived.

Leontine and her brother, George, who she said as a child "was the most handsome and intelligent boy she knew," were raised in a religious home. Her parents attended St. Paul Methodist Church regularly. She liked music, so her mother decided to give her lessons, and Leontine learned to play the piano at a very early age. Her parents soon felt that she was a child prodigy because of her aptitude, and sacrificed many necessities to continue her piano lessons. By the time Leontine was ten years old, she was playing at all the church Sunday school affairs and at many social functions. She began to sing in the church choir and received many compliments on her clear, sweet voice.

Leontine went to Oak Park Vocational High School in Laurel, Mississippi, and was graduated in 1944. She had decided to become a music teacher when she entered the College of Educational Arts at Wilberforce University in Ohio, where she went at the insistence of her parents. They did not want her to go to a college in the South, as they felt that opportunities were greater in the North.

While at Wilberforce, Leontine took part in school plays and musicals and the president, Dr. Charles Wesley, was so impressed with her voice that he suggested she make application for a scholarship to the Juilliard School of Music in New York. Leontine received the scholarship, and she said, "Neither my father nor I had enough money to continue my training, and I was afraid for a while I would have to sing in night clubs." But Mrs. Elizabeth Chisholm, a very good friend, in whose home my aunt worked in Laurel, Mississippi, went to my father and offered to pay my living expenses so I could accept the scholarship."

In 1948, Leontine earned her B.A. degree from Wilberforce and enrolled at Juilliard. For four years she studied under the former concert singer, Florence Page Kimball, who has been her teacher, advisor, and friend ever since. After Leontine sang in the student production of Verdi's *Falstaff*, the composer, Virgil Thompson, selected her for the role of St. Cecilia in his *Four Saints in Three Acts*, which was presented on Broadway for two weeks in April, 1952. She received her first professional check for her part, and says, "everything started to happen at once for some weird reason or other."

Her appearance on Broadway was so successful that George Gershwin granted her an audition and after hearing her sing "Summertime," he gave her the feminine lead in *Porgy and Bess*. The revival of this opera with Miss Price was played to packed houses for two years, 1952 and 1953, in Dallas, Philadelphia, Washington, and then abroad in Berlin, Paris, and London. Peter Hume of the *Washington Post* wrote, "Leontyne [she had changed the spelling of her name for professional reasons] Price sings the most exciting Bess we have heard and will no doubt spend a long time in this role. But when she is not available for other music, she will have a dramatic career. Her acting is as fiery as her singing."

Miss Price began laying the groundwork for a career in grand opera by studying and giving concerts. Her schedule with *Porgy and Bess* was arranged so that she could accept invitations to sing at the Metropolitan Museum of Modern Arts in New York, and at Constitution Hall in Washington, D.C. In October, 1953, Sam Barber asked her to sing his "Hermit Songs" at their première at the Library of Congress, which was a big success. She then flew to Rome to sing at the International Conference of Contemporary Music, the only American invited to perform.

Leontyne made her Town Hall debut on November 14, 1954, before an appreciative audience and press. Many of the musical critics came to see how she would bridge the gap between light opera and grand opera, and Jay Harrison of the *New York Herald Tribune* wrote of her as "a personality that literally spills charm over the footlights." Maestro Peter Herman Adler, who was the musical director of the NBC-TV opera, was particularly interested and impressed with her performance. He asked her to sing the part of Floria in the

TV production of Puccini's *Tosca*. Her performance in February, 1955, overshadowed the others in the cast with her full, high notes and dramatic acting. She then received leading roles in other NBC-TV productions: Mozart's *The Magic Flute* in 1956; in 1957, Francis Poulenc's *Dialogues of the Carmelites;* and in 1960, Mozart's *Don Giovanni.*

Miss Price made her onstage grand opera debut at the San Francisco Opera, singing Poulenc's *Dialogues of the Carmelites.* She has interpreted Leonora in Verdi's *Il Trovatore;* Donna Elviar in *Don Giovanni;* and the leading part in Carl Orff's *The Wise Maiden.* In Chicago, with the Lyric Opera, Leontyne sang Massenet's *Thaïs* and Puccini's *Turandot* in 1959, and in 1960, *Aida* and *Madame Butterfly.*

At the request of Conductor Herbert von Karajan, Miss Price took the role of Aida at the Vienna State Opera. This was followed by another performance at the Verona Arena under Maestro Tullio Serafin, a tour of Yugoslavia, and recitals at the Brussels' World Fair. She was soloist in Beethoven's *Missa Solemnis* at the Salzburg Festival, and sang in Covent Garden, London. In May, 1960, Leontyne sang *Aida* without any rehearsals at Milan's Teatro alla Scala, and was awarded "bravas" by her audience.

Miss Price received her first offer from the Metropolitan Opera in 1959. Her ambition was realized! But she turned it down because it was the wrong kind of contract and at the wrong time. She says, "I was doing something else at the time, and said to myself, Oh, well, I can't go now, so I guess I'll never make the Met." But she was wrong about this, for her unremitting hard work in concert halls, opera houses, recording studios, and practicing and coaching sessions won her rave notices. After she sang Donna Anna in Salzburg, she was again invited to the Metropolitan Opera and offered a "decent" contract.

In January, 1961, Leontyne Price made her debut as Leonora in *Il Trovatore* for the Metropolitan Opera, and when she had interpreted the difficult role, the critics agreed that she had "scored one of the greatest operatic triumphs in recent years." She repeated her success in later roles at the Met in *Madame Butterfly, Don Giovanni* and *Turandot.* On October 23, 1961, Leontyne opened the 1961–62 season at the Metropolitan Opera in the role of Minnie in *La Fanciulla del West,* Puccini's opera about the California Gold Rush.

Miss Price acknowledges the encouragement she has received from her parents, the Chisholm family, Florence Page Kimball, her accompanist David Garvey, and teachers, throughout the years. She often returns to Laurel, Mississippi, where she says she can be "just Leontyne," and where her career is a source of local pride.

In 1963, Leontyne gave a recital in her home town to an unsegregated audience. She said, "The people in Laurel and neighboring towns around, who knew my parents and me as a little child, suddenly felt as if I were a part of them, and unconsciously they didn't care whether they sat next to each other or not. They just wanted to hear me sing."

Miss Price has made numerous recordings of her operatic arias, French and German art songs, and was selected by *Mademoiselle* as one of the ten outstanding women in 1955, for her performance in *Tosca.* Her RCA Victor recording of Bizet's famed opera *Carmen* was named "Record of the Year" by newspaper and magazine record review critics representing Italy, Germany, and the United States. She is a member of the American Guild of Musical Artists, Actors' Equity Association, and The American Federation of Television and Radio Artists, as well as Sigma Alpha Iota and Delta Sigma Theta. In April, 1965, the Italian government conferred upon her the Order of Merit of the Italian republic.

On August 31, 1952, she married William C. Warfield, the concert baritone, who co-starred with her in *Porgy and Bess*. They own an attractive house in Greenwich Village, where she enjoys entertaining her family and friends. Her hobbies are interior decorating, record collecting, and walking her two pet poodles.

Although Miss Price thoroughly enjoys her success, she is anything but the stereotyped prima donna. She sings Italian, yet she is a Negro. Too much has been made of the artist's racial and geographical origin, because origin is supposed to determine something of the style of vocal delivery. But there is nothing whatsoever of this special manner about the way Leontyne sings the music assigned to her. She has one of the most highly cultivated voices of the century, with a technique that is almost unexcelled.

On January 2, 1966, Leontyne Price was awarded the Spingarn Medal "in recognition of her divinely inspired talent, in tribute to her extraordinary achievement as the outstanding soprano of our era, and in appreciation to her priceless contribution as artist, citizen, and person, to the continuing crusade for justice, equality and understanding among the peoples of the world." The presentation was made by Rudolf Bing, general manager of the Metropolitan Opera Company. On September 16, 1966, she had the unique honor of singing the role of Cleopatra in Samuel Barber's *Antony* and *Cleo-*

patra at the opening of the new home of the Metropolitan Opera in Lincoln Center in New York.

Miss Price feels that her work is just beginning. She says, "I want to sing for a long time."

PAUL ROBESON

Baritone Singer - Actor

[1898–   ]

THE RICH, communicative sound of a distinguished Negro baritone which made itself heard around the world was the voice of Paul Robeson. Although he preferred folk songs to classical music, his rendition of English, Hebrew, Russian, and German folk songs, often sung in the original tongue, portrayed the deep sincerity that made him the most famous male singer of Negro spirituals of his day.

Paul Robeson was born in Princeton, New Jersey, on April 9, 1898, the son of Anna Louise (Bustill) and William Drew Robeson. His father was a runaway slave who put himself through Lincoln University and became a Methodist minister. His mother died when Paul was six years old, and his father moved to Westfield, and later to Somerville, New Jersey.

Paul attended school in Somerville and showed a remarkable aptitude for learning. In high school, he was not only a brilliant scholar, but an all-around athlete. In 1915, he won a state scholarship to Rutgers University and became the third Negro to enter this historic seat of learning. He made an outstanding record there, winning the freshman prize in oratory and the sophomore and junior prizes in extemporaneous speaking. He became a member of the debating team and a speaker at commencement, in addition to winning letters in track, football, basketball, and baseball. He was chosen All-American end in 1917 and 1918.

Robeson received his B.A. from Rutgers in 1919 and went to Columbia to take his LL.B. He financed his own law studies by playing week-end football games. When he left Columbia, he was taken into the office of Louis W. Stotesbury, a Rutgers man, and a prominent New York lawyer. Here Paul met his first experience with race prejudice because some members of the firm objected to his presence. Reluctantly, he left law practice.

Paul had taken part in an amateur play while at Columbia, and Eugene O'Neill, who had been in the audience, was impressed with his acting ability. Later, when O'Neill wrote *Emperor Jones,* he offered Paul the part in his play. Robeson refused this leading role because he felt he was not ready for serious acting, but soon afterward consented to play in *Taboo.* He appeared with Margaret Wycherly in the United States and with Mrs. Patrick Campbell in the London production. Paul then consented to do *Emperor Jones* in New York, and when it went to London, the English performance proved to be such a triumph that he decided to give up law permanently for the stage.

He received very high critical comment for his acting and singing ability. His performance in *All God's Chillun Got Wings* caused Laurence Stallings of the *New York World* to write, "There is no doubt about Robeson's ability. The man brings a genius to the piece. What other player on the American stage has his great, taunt body, the singing grace and litheness of the man who with a football under his arm sidestepped half the broken fields of the East? And who has a better voice for tragedy than this actor whose tone and resonance suggest nothing so much as the dusky, poetic quality of a Negro spiritual, certainly the most tragic utterances in American life?"

Paul's great success in these two plays increased his interest in the theatre. He stated, "If someday I can play *Othello* as Shakespeare wrote it, bring to the stage the nobility of sympathy and understanding Shakespeare put into the play, I will make the audience know that he was not just a dark, foreign brute of three hundred years ago in far-off Venice, who murdered a beautiful, innocent white girl, but that Othello was a fine, noble, tragic human figure, ruined by the very human weakness of jealousy."

Later, in London, and again in New York, Paul was able to realize his ambitions to play Othello. His portrayal of the Moor in Margaret Webster's Broadway production was enough to establish him for all time as one of the outstanding personalities of the American stage. His fame spread all over the world, and he became as well known in London and Moscow as in New York.

In 1925, Robeson was invited to give a concert of Negro music in New York in conjunction with pianist, Lawrence Brown. The music critic of the *New York Times* wrote of it, "Mr. Robeson is a singer of genuine power. His Negro spirituals have the ring of a revivalist, they hold in them a world of religious experience; it is a cry from the depths, this rich, humanism that touches the heart, sung by one man, they voiced the sorrows and hopes of a people."

The same year, Paul went to England where he was received warmly. From 1926 to 1928 he did concert tours in

America and in 1928 played *Show Boat* in London. In 1929, Paul made his first film appearance in *Borderline* with a mixed cast, and in 1933, he made his first talking film version of *Emperor Jones*, which was recognized as an artistic success. He returned to Europe, where he starred in Alexander Korda's *Sanders of the River*.

It was while he was in Columbia Law School that Paul met and married Eslanda Cardoza Goode. She, like Paul, was a brilliant scholar. She was then in the Medical School of Columbia and subsequently went on to become an outstanding writer and anthropologist, specializing in Africa.

Because of the racial discrimination Paul met with in the United States, he decided to live abroad. In the course of his travels, he visited Soviet Russia, and admired many things about that country. In 1935, when he returned to the Soviet Union on a concert tour, Paul took his son with him and left him there to be educated.

Robeson has been awarded a score of honorary degrees from distinguished colleges and universities, including Humboldt University of Berlin, in 1960. On the occasion of the award of Honorary Degree of Doctor of Human Letters from Morehouse College in 1943, Dr. Benjamin E. Mays, the president, stated: "Your singing is a declaration of faith. You sing as if God Almighty sent you into the world to advocate the cause of the common man in song. You are truly the people's artist."

In 1964, *Freedomways Magazine* welcomed Paul Robeson back home after a long absence. It stated, "Phi Beta Kappa scholar, Spingarn Medalist, and above all, sterling fighter in the cause of Freedom, Human Dignity, and World Peace— the noblest ideals of man—Paul Robeson was the inspiration and idol of a whole generation of Negro youth who grew up to adulthood in the early struggles of the CIO and New Deal. Many a day, Paul Robeson was with them on their picket lines, speaking at their mass meetings, and giving of his cultural talents in benefit concerts. Because of these activities, Robeson became a target of 'McCarthyism' and the racists succeeded in getting his passport withdrawn for several years. However, world public opinion knew and admired this great Negro American."

Paul himself once said, "If, with my music, I can re-create for an audience the great sadness of the Negro slave in, for instance, 'Sometimes I Feel Like a Motherless Child,' or if I can make them know the strong, gallant convict of the chain gang, make them feel his thirst, understand his naive boasting about his strength, feel the brave gaiety and sadness in 'Water Boy,' or if I can explain to them the simple, divine faith of the Negro in 'Weepin' Mary,' then I shall increase their knowledge and understanding of my people. They will sense that we are moved by the same emotions, have the same beliefs, the same longings, that, in fact, we are all human together. That will be something worth working for, something worth doing."

Paul Robeson is respected because of his art, vision, and understanding. He will be remembered for having fought for the world's peoples with his songs.

BILL "BOJANGLES" ROBINSON

Dancer-Actor

[1878–1949]

LUTHER ROBINSON was born in Richmond, Virginia, on May 25, 1878, the son of a machine shop worker, Maxwell Robinson, and a choir singer, Maria Robinson. Both his parents died when he was a baby and he was raised by his grandmother, an emancipated slave.

He soon grew tired of being teased about the name of Luther, and decided to change names with his brother, who put up a fight, but lost. So from an early age, Luther became known as Bill Robinson, and his brother later changed the name of Luther to Percy.

Bill's formal education ended soon after he was six years old. He had learned to dance to earn nickels and dimes at Richmond beer gardens, and when he was eight years old, Bill begged rides to Washington, D.C., where he worked in racing stables and danced on the streets for whatever money was given him.

The year 1906 marked Robinson's real start on the road to fame. When a show called *The South Before the War* came through town, little Bill joined it and traveled all over the country. He was a small, bright-eyed, brown boy, and his flying feet added humor to the old plantation scenes.

For the next ten years Bill went about the land with various traveling shows, then divided his time between night club entertaining and dancing on the stage. He played big-time vaudeville as long as it lasted; from *Blackbirds of 1928* to *Brown Buddies*, he danced many a show to success. Robinson was considered the "dean" of all American buck-and-wing dancers.

Bill had two vices—playing poker and eating large quantities of ice cream. He could eat four to five quarts of ice cream a day. At one poker game he won his famous nickname. After winning a great deal of money, he did a "victory" dance in the streets. One of the losers, Des Williams, exclaimed, "Bojangles, that's what he is; he's Bojangles," which, loosely translated, means "happy-go-lucky." From that time on, the nickname stayed with him.

"Bojangles" stopped dancing long enough to serve his country in two wars, the Spanish-American and the First World War. After he was mustered out of the service at the end of World War One, his twinkling feet earned him membership in the country's outstanding dance organizations. He was made an honorary member of The Dancing Masters' Association of America, and won first prize four times in a row in the National Dance Contests sponsored by McFadden Magazine. He received many honors and appeared at thousands of benefits for good causes during his lifetime.

It is not generally known, but at one time Bill Robinson had distinguished himself by holding the record for backward running. He covered the distance of seventy-five yards in eight and one-fifth seconds.

"Bojangles" went to Hollywood in 1930, and between the

years 1930 and 1939 he made fourteen motion pictures for major studios. The most popular movies were those in which he co-starred with his favorite little actress, Shirley Temple. With her, Bill made such hits as *The Little Colonel* and *Rebecca of Sunnybrook Farm*. He taught her many intricate dance steps, and together they became a number-one box office attraction.

The Hot Mikado marked Robinson's return to the stage in 1939. This musical version of the opera became one of the outstanding features at the New York World's Fair during its stay.

The stair tap is probably "Bojangles'" outstanding contribution to dancing. There are several versions of how the step originated, but Bill's favorite is attributed to a dream. "I was being made a lord by the King of England," he said, "and he was standing at the head of a flight of stairs. Rather than walk, I danced up the stairs to receive my lordship." However the step began, Robinson is remembered for this particular feat in his long dancing career, and many dancers since have tried to imitate his technique.

"He expressed as much beauty with his feet as a singer does with his voice," a critic once said. Robinson himself said, "I hear the music, and something comes into my head which I just send down to my feet. And that's all there is to it. They just won't be still after that!"

Once when "Bojangles" was asked by a reporter how he could dance so long at a time, he replied, "I don't smoke and I don't drink, and dancing never makes me tired. I can keep right on doing it for hours and never get winded. I have no feeling for that slapstick dancing which a lot of people do. They have no respect for their feet. No piano player would treat his hands that way and I make music with my feet, so I just treat 'em with great respect. That's the reason they can do this," he said, as he invented a new step.

Bill Robinson was married to the former Fannie S. Clay, and replied to a comment from a friend, "I've been married more than twenty years—and all that time to the same woman."

"Bojangles" made New York his adopted home and spent his later life there. His popularity became universal. One of the greatest honors bestowed upon him was his admittance into the organization known as the Grand Street Boys. On the occasion of his sixtieth birthday in 1938, the Grand Street Boys held a party in his honor at which ex-Mayor Walker referred to him as "probably the greatest dancer in the world today."

For fifty years "Bojangles" danced across the stages of America. His was one of the longest continuous careers in the history of show business. He made records and tap-danced on radio and television, also. To honor his sixtieth year on the stage, Mayor William O'Dwyer of New York City proclaimed that April 26, 1946, be celebrated as "Bill Robinson Day." Many celebrities paid homage to him on that day.

When Bill "Bojangles" Robinson died on November 25, 1949, thousands of dignitaries from all walks of life turned out to pay him tribute. The funeral procession went down Broadway, passing many of the theatres where he had danced, and the bands played the tunes to which he had tapped.

"BERT" WILLIAMS
Comedian - Actor
[1876–1922]

"BERT" WILLIAMS, whose full name was Egbert Austin Williams, was born in New Providence, Nassau, Bahama Islands. He was taken to New York at the age of two by his father, who was a papier-mâché maker. Later they moved to Riverside, California, where the boy grew up and was graduated from high school. At first he studied civil engineering in San Francisco, but soon his interest turned to the theatre. His first theatrical experience was with a mountebank minstrel company that played the mining and lumber camps in that section.

In 1895, Williams joined George Walker in a partnership that lasted until the death of Walker in 1909. This team of Williams and Walker became famous, appearing initially in New York in 1896 and 1897 at Tony Pastor's and Koster and Biol's. In 1900, they appeared in *The Song of Ham*, a musical farce which ran for two years, with Williams as a burnt-faced comic and Walker as a well-dressed dandy. Then came their great success, *In Dahomey*. It opened in 1902 with music by Will Marion Cook, lyrics by Paul Laurence Dunbar, and booked by Jess Ships. This show went to London the following year where it played a command performance for King Edward VII at Buckingham Palace. They then headed their own production company, bringing out such shows as *The Policy Players, Bandanna Land,* and *Abyssinia,* which set a record at that time by running ten weeks on Broadway.

After George Walker died, Bert Williams continued as a featured performer in otherwise all-white Broadway musicals. In 1910, he signed a long-term contract with the Ziegfeld Follies where he and Fannie Brice made their first appearance in the fourth edition of the famous show. He thus became the first Negro to be featured with Broadway's theatrical elite. Later he toured American cities for ten years in various editions of that review, singing and recording such comical songs as his own "Nobody," Irving Berlin's "Woodman Spare That Tree," or Will Cook's "O Death, Where is Thy Sting?"

Though he appeared in blackface in the theatre as a slouching, careless, dialect-speaking, unlucky Negro for whom everything went wrong, in real life, Bert Williams was a tall, distinguished-looking man, with carriage as straight as a soldier. He spoke perfect English. He always sang in a mournful bass voice and represented himself as a lazy, good-for-nothing fellow, a part that he initiated. It was much imitated later, most notably by the radio comedians who produced Amos 'n' Andy, and Eddie Cantor on the stage.

Present-day comedians avoid poking fun at any race by overemphasis on conventional notions about them, by using dialect or other racial characteristics. The amusing characterizations by Red Skelton and similar comedians stem directly, however, from the successful creations of Bert Williams.

In contrast to his stage personality, Bert Williams was a serious student whose interests extended over many areas. He was familiar with the works of Voltaire, Tom Paine, Goethe, Plato, Schopenhauer, and other philosophers. His mastery of the art of pantomime and his unique monologue styles have never been equaled by any other comedian, Negro or white.

Eddie Cantor said of Bert Williams, "As a performer, he was close to genius. As a man, he was everything the rest of us would like to have been. As a friend, he was without envy or jealousy."

Honors that accrued to him included membership in the Waverly Lodge of Masons. He was a member of Actors Equity Association and a Captain in the Eighth Regiment of the National Guard of Illinois.

Billboard of March 11, 1922, wrote of him, "E. A. Williams, known to the theatrical profession as 'Bert' Williams, and regarded by many as the greatest comedian on the American stage, died at his home, March 4, of pneumonia. He collapsed on the stage in Detroit, Monday, February 7, while appearing in *Under the Bamboo Tree* and was taken to New York, Thursday, when it was found he was suffering from pneumonia. Blood transfusion was ordered, but Williams failed to react."

So passed one of the best-beloved figures of the American stage and the first American of African descent to make an important success in the theatre.

THOMAS "FATS" WALLER
Jazz Pianist
[1904–1943]

THE CHUBBY fourteen-year-old boy, round as a butterball, sat down at the magnificent pipe organ on the stage of the Lincoln Theatre in Harlem, New York. The manager had invited him to test the new $10,000 Wurlitzer Grand. "Go ahead, Fats," he said. "Pull out all the stops and stab those keys!"

That spring afternoon in 1918, the young musician, Thomas Waller, played his heart out—hymns, popular songs, and jazz tunes. He then ran all the way home to tell the good news to his brothers and sisters, but his father was very upset and said, "I forbid you to play jazz. It is music from the devil's workshop."

Thomas Wright Waller was born May 21, 1904, in New York City, the sixth child of Edward Martin Waller and Adelaide (Lockett) Waller. There were twelve children in all born to the Wallers, but only five survived. Thomas was reared in a very religious atmosphere; his father was the minister of the Abyssinian Baptist Church, one of the largest Negro congregations in New York, and his mother was the leading soloist with the choir. The Bible was read every day within the family circle, and each child knew by heart many passages from the Scripture. There also was much singing in the home. The children often awoke to the sound of their mother's melodious voice in the kitchen as she prepared breakfast, and after dinner a song-fest was held in which everyone joined in singing the hymns familiar to them.

Little Thomas began taking on weight so rapidly that soon his friends were calling him "Fats," a nickname which stayed with him all his life. When he was six years old, his favorite pastime was pretending to play the piano. He put two straight-backed chairs side by side and knelt in front of them with his fingers poised, gliding his hands back and forth across the edges of the seats. He kept perfect rhythm as though he were actually playing a tune. His older brother, Bob, after watching him at this for some time, asked if he would like to have a real piano, and Fats replied gleefully that he would. The family decided to try to get one, and after making arrangements through an uncle to help finance it, a new Waters Upright was delivered to the Waller home.

For a while Fats and his younger sister, Naomi, just ran their fingers over the keys, as there was no money for music lessons. Gradually Fats began picking out tunes which he made up, until a teacher, Miss Perry, was hired to give the children lessons. The piano lessons soon became uninteresting to them, and when Miss Perry asked why they did not pay more attention, Fats told her he just wanted to "play music, not scales." He would ask her to play a piece, watch intently, then go home and play the entire melody by ear. The music lessons were soon discontinued.

Fats loved music and it came as naturally to him as breathing. By the time he was ten years old, he was playing the organ in his father's church each week for Sunday school. In 1919, he quit high school to take a job as pianist with a vaudeville troupe, against his father's wishes. While in Boston, at the age of fifteen, he wrote his first song called "Boston Blues," the title of which was later changed to "Squeeze Me." The lyrics were done by his new-found friend, Spencer Williams, and "Squeeze Me" immediately became a hit tune.

Upon his return to New York after his tour with the troupe, Fats was given the job of playing the big, beautiful pipe organ at the Lincoln Theatre where he had tried out for the manager less than two years before. He became an instant favorite at the theatre, not only because of his musical talents, but for his bubbly humor and comments, improvised on the spot, which kept the audience laughing.

One night after his performance, James P. Johnson, dean of the Harlem pianists, commended Fats on the way he played the organ, but said to him, "I think you have what it takes to make a great piano man. A good piano man needs a powerful left hand to develop a bass style. I'd like to teach you a few tricks." Fats was delighted, and from that night on he was at the Johnson home at all hours, practicing and banging away with his left hand on the piano. In addition to emphasizing the importance of his left hand, Mr. Johnson also taught Fats the secrets of style and symmetry, and how to repeat a phrase so as to add tension and excitement to the piece. But it was Fats' humor and whimsy in the trills and grace notes that finally became his trademark.

The famous band leader, Fletcher Henderson, invited him to join his great band, but Fats stayed with him only a short time, for he longed to travel. He went to Chicago, where he became the pianist in Erskine Tate's orchestra, playing at the

Vendome Theatre on the celebrated State Street. Louis Armstrong was also with the Tate band at that time, and Louis and Fats were a drawing attraction. The theatre was crowded to capacity for every performance.

In 1926, Fats toured with Bessie Smith, the famous blues singer, as her accompanist, and that same year, he and James P. Johnson, his instructor, wrote a full-length musical review, *Shuffle Along*. It opened on February 27, 1928, at Daly's 63rd Street Theatre in New York. An instant success, the show delighted critics and the audience alike. Also in 1926, Fats married Anita Rutherford, and they had two sons, Maurice and Ronald, who were a constant source of delight to Fats.

Original tunes sprang from Waller's mind and fingers with great ease. With Andy Razaf, his most successful collaborator, who did the lyrics, he wrote the entire score for *Hot Chocolate*, a musical hit review of 1928. Fats did the music for a show called *Junior Blackbirds*, and each year for a long time afterward, a production of Lew Leslie's *Blackbirds* played to packed houses in theatres throughout Harlem.

Fats wrote a composition, "Jitterbug Waltz," in ten minutes while his thirteen-year-old son, Maurice, looked on in astonishment at the ease with which his father could create a tune. Some of the famous Waller melodies are "Squeeze Me," "Blue Turning Grey over You," "Keeping Out of Mischief Now," "Black and Blue," "I've Got a Feeling I'm Fallin'," "Honeysuckle Rose," and "Ain't Misbehavin'."

In 1928, W. C. Handy sponsored and conducted a sixty-voice choir and thirty-piece orchestra at Carnegie Hall in a concert called "Musical History of the Negro." Fats Waller was featured in this performance along with J. Rosamond Johnson, Will Marion Cook, and many other distinguished musicians. He played "Beale Street Blues" on the organ with orchestral accompaniment, and at the piano, a rhapsody entitled "Yamekraw" written by James P. Johnson, just as Mr. Johnson would have played it himself. His former instructor had coached Fats well. The concert was a rousing success both artistically and financially.

Fats Waller toured Europe with his friend, Spencer Williams, who had written the lyrics to his first hit tune, spending much of his time in Paris. He played to large audiences in Cabaine Cuban, Gavarnies' Melody's Bar, L'Enfer, and Boudon's Cafe. While in Paris he met Marcel Dupre, the eminent European organist, who took Fats to Notre Dame Cathedral, where he and Fats took turns playing the great organ. It was an unforgettable moment in Waller's life, and brought back many memories of his youth.

Upon his return to the United States, he formed a jazz combo, a sextet called "Fats Waller and His Rhythm Boys," that became an immediate success on records and in personal appearances. One of the biggest commercial hits with the combo was his own original tune, "I'm Gonna Sit Right Down and Write Myself a Letter." They traveled throughout the country, making one-night stands and sometimes stayed in one place for a week at a time by popular request. One of their most notable engagements during the mid-thirties was at the Panther Room of the Sherman Hotel in Chicago. Fats, with his derby hat cocked over one ear, played the piano and made bright sayings which became bywords to a capacity audience.

In 1938, he revisited Europe, this time with his manager, Ed Kirkeby, who had made arrangements for Fats to play in Scotland and England. The musical column "Spotlight on

Glasgow Shows" in the *Evening News* had this to say of his performance: "Into the Victorian setting at the Empire Theatre last night stepped no prim little miss of a vanished century, but the dynamic 285-pound King of Swing. The contrast between the mature staging and the ultra-modern performance may have been accidental, but it did not need any soft lights to make Waller's programme sweet music. His playing was nothing if not soothing, and even if there may be many of us who lay no claim to an understanding of 'swing,' the last charge that anyone could lay at Waller's door is that of being noisy or raucous. Fats, in the words of his own composition, was not misbehavin'." He had thus made a big impression on the music lovers of Glasgow, Scotland.

When Fats arrived in London, he went to the Palladium, where he saw on the great electric sign of the world-famous theatre, FATS WALLER—WORLD'S GREATEST RHYTHM PIANIST. That night, after his performance, he received thunderous applause and had to take curtain call after curtain call. Walter Winchell wrote in the *New York Daily Mirror:* "The present controversy between Benny Goodman and Louis Armstrong over the title 'King of Swing' is belittled by musicians . . . they contend that neither of them plays an instrument of rhythm. . . . Fats Waller, however, 'toys' with a piano and if we were a committee of one to decide matters, Fats would certainly get the title." While in London, Waller wrote a serious composition *London Suite,* which consisted of six pieces, to commemorate his successful engagements there.

Back home in America, Hollywood called to Fats to play in several movies. In 1942, he disbanded his jazz combo and went to Hollywood, starring in such films as *Hooray for Love, King of Burlesque,* and *Stormy Weather.* He won most of the honors in the latter with his catch phrase, "One never knows, do one?" which was not in the original script.

At the age of thirty-nine, Fats Waller, who had made such a success with his musical talents, wanted just one dream fulfilled. This was a concert at Carnegie Hall, where he had played with the W. C. Handy spectacular. At last a solo concert was arranged for him, and Carnegie Hall was packed that night, and many were turned away. Fats was a little nervous at first, but as soon as his fingers touched the piano, he warmed to the feel of the keys, and played with all his heart the music he had longed to bring to the public. When he had finished, the audience cheered as it seldom had done before. His dream was realized!

The internationally known jazz composer, pianist, and band leader died of pneumonia on December 15, 1943, while on a train en route from California to New York. He left behind more than a thousand records, scores of original tunes, a piano style all his own, and the sound of laughter and banter in his voice.

His biography, appropriately titled *Ain't Misbehavin'*, by Ed Kirkeby, his friend and manager, was published in 1966 by Dodd, Mead & Company.

INDEX

CHARLEMAE ROLLINS began her valuable work as a librarian in The Chicago Public Library in March, 1927. She was in charge of the Children's Department in The George C. Hall Branch from January, 1932, to July, 1963, when she retired. The fine help she offered in her chosen field and the wide and enduring influence that she had on the reading tastes and enthusiasms of the young people whom she served so well have been captured by one of those who "grew up in our Branch Library" and happily shared in this generous heritage. Gwendolyn Brooks, the only Negro Pulitzer Prize Winner, wrote this poem as a tribute to Charlemae Hill Rollins:

> Her gift is long delayed.
> And even now is paid
> In insufficient measure.
> Rhymeful reverence,
> For such excellence,
> Is microscopic treasure.
> NOTHING is enough
> For one who gave us clarity—
> Who gave us sentience—
> Who gave us definition—
> Who gave us her vision.

Mrs. Rollins has taught in such diverse places as Fisk University, Nashville, Tennessee; Human Relations Workshop, San Francisco State College, California; Department of Library Science, Rosary College, River Forest, Illinois; and a class in Children's Literature at Roosevelt University, Chicago, Illinois.

She has received the following special honors: American Brotherhood Award of the National Conference of Christians and Jews, 1952; Library Letter Award of the American Library Association, 1953; Grolier Society Award of ALA, 1955; Woman of the Year of Zeta Phi Beta, 1956; Honorable Member, Phi Delta Kappa (Teachers Sorority), 1959; Good American Award of The Chicago Committee of One Hundred, 1962; Negro Centennial Awards (in three areas), 1963; and Children's Reading Round Table Award, 1963.

While writing books and contributing articles to such periodicals as *ALA Bulletin, Junior Libraries, Elementary English*, etc., etc., Mrs. Rollins has found time to serve as President of Children's Services Division of ALA, 1957–58; Chairman, Children's Section of Illinois Library Association, 1953–54; Chairman, Newbery-Caldecott Awards Committee of ALA, 1956–57; and Chairman, Elementary Section of Illinois Unit of Catholic Library Association, 1953–54.